Copyright © HTJ Capital, LLC. All rights reserved. No part of this publication may be reproduced, distributed, or transmitted in any form, or by any means, including photography, recording, or other electronic or mechanical methods, without the prior written permission of the publisher, except in the case of brief quotations embodied in reviews and certain other non-commercial uses permitted by the copyright law.

In response to IRS Circular 230 requirements, we advise that any discussion of Federal tax issues in our publications and products, or in third party publications and products on our platforms, are not intended to be used and may not, in fact, be used to avoid any penalties under the Internal Revenue Code, or to promote, market, or recommend, any transaction, or subject addressed therein.

Table of Contents

- Table of Contents 5
- Foreword 7
- Legal Disclaimer 8
- Introduction 9
- How to Use This Book 10
- Chapter 1 - Post Pandemic Actions for International Entrepreneurs and Expats 13
  - Review Your Portfolio of Citizenships and Residencies 14
    - Portugal as my Plan B 16
    - Focus on quality jurisdictions for secondary residencies or citizenship. Not just tax mitigation. 19
  - Be Prepared for Reduced Freedoms of Movement 21
  - Acceleration of Remote Working and Learning 23
    - Remote Work Is More Prevalent in Certain Areas 25
    - Commercial Real Estate 26
    - Learning and Development 28
  - Rising Importance of Third-Party Professional Services such as Family Offices 30
    - The Many Disciplines of a 'Family Office' 32
    - Legacy Planning and Management 32
    - Lifestyle Management 33
- Chapter 2 - Lessons from the Past 34
  - Lessons from 1918 Spanish Flu 34
  - Lessons from the 2002 SARS 36
  - Lessons from the 2009 H1N1 / Swine Flu Pandemic 39
- Chapter 3 - Trends before the Pandemic 42
  - Income and Wealth Inequality 42
  - Economic Nationalism 48
  - Slowing Global GDP growth. Focus on Asia 50
- Chapter 4 - Trends to Watch in The Post Pandemic World 52
  - Economic Responses 52
  - Pumping the Brakes - Periodic Lockdowns 56
  - Rising Inequality 58
    - Social Inequality within Nations 58
    - Inequality Between and Among Nations 62

    ASEAN as an Example 64
        But is Inequality a Bad Thing? 68
  Entrepreneurship is dead. Long live entrepreneurship 69
  Rising Economic Nationalism and Conscious Uncoupling 74
    Supply Chains 76
    Impact on Foreign Direct Investment (FDI) 77
    Protectionism 79
    The Decoupling of "Chimerica" 81
Chapter 5 - Conclusion - The "Shut In" Economy 83
  Recession vs Depression 86
PostScript - Remember the End Game 93
  (i)   Flag Theory - Diversify Your Lifestyle 94
  (ii) Choose Tax Systems that Work For You 94
  (iii) Choose to Live Where YOU Want 97
  (iv) You can Bank Internationally 100

Foreword

In claiming that the pandemic has created "nothing new", merely accelerated pre-existing socio-economic trends and conditions, Derren Joseph presents a list of carefully thought out steps that international entrepreneurs can take to help protect their wealth.

Drawing on lessons learned from the 1918 Spanish Flu, 2002 SARS and 2009 HINI / Swine Flu Pandemic he plots a likely course of how the "new" normal may play out. These include things that we will all have to get used to, both in the short-term and perhaps even a different way of doing things. Health care for sure will get more than a passing glance when it comes to choosing places of residence, as will rights of entry.

Looking at trends that have been growing for a number of years, the divergence in income and wealth between rich and poor will only increase at an even faster rate, and this will likely include countries too. Economic nationalism that has been gaining a foothold in Europe and the US – think Brexit and Trump – will become a flavor of the month as nations try to make the most of what they have.

The slump that people have been talking about, it's arrived and now it's a matter of whether it's a sharp V or a slow U in shape. Looking at the prospects of Asia, Dereen comes up with something of a surprise as a country to quickly recover.

It's pointers for the future that we need, though, and in Trends to Watch in the Post Pandemic World he unveils his thoughts on what may come to pass.

As an international entrepreneur, myself, as well as CEO of an accounting and consulting firm, there is much with which I concur. There are also a few twists that I wish I'd thought of myself!

James S. Kallman

CEO Moores Rowland Indonesia

Website: www.moores-rowland.com/

Legal Disclaimer

It is important to note that the views expressed in this book are that of the writer and do not reflect the views of the publishers or any other affiliates in any way or form.

This book is made available by the writer and publishers for educational purposes only, as well as to give general information and provide a general understanding of certain economic and social factors.

It is not to provide you with specific legal or financial advice. By purchasing and reading this book, you understand that there is no attorney-client relationship, nor any other client-advisory relationship of any kind, between yourself, the writer or publishers. This book should not be used as a substitute, in any way, for competent legal or financial advice, from a licensed professional in your area or state.

Under no circumstances shall the writer or publisher, or anyone else involved in the production of this book, be held liable for any indirect, incidental, consequential, special or exemplary damages arising out of, or in connection with, your access, use, or inability to use the content of this book.

Enjoy the book

Deandre T Joseph

Bio:
After spending four (4) years in Singapore and South-East Asia, Deandre T Joseph is now based in Miami, Florida. He has a UK Law Degree, is an Associate with Moores Rowland Tax Consultants and is enrolled at the University of Miami School of Law. Deandre T Joseph works with US exposed entrepreneurs doing business internationally.

Email: legal@AdvancedAmericanTax.com
LinkedIn: https://www.linkedin.com/in/deandrejoseph/
Website: www.htj.tax

Introduction

My name is Derren Joseph and I am a part of a finance practice that works with entrepreneurs and expats doing business internationally. I am frequently asked for opinions that extend beyond taxation. It is not unusual for me to spend time with my clients and colleagues discussing socioeconomic trends and their impact on specific geographies and industries.

The present pandemic is perhaps the single most important event of our lives. It will shape our world in unimaginable ways. I wrote this book in the hope that it may help entrepreneurs like you and my clients. Entrepreneurs who operate internationally and must now pivot and retool themselves and their teams for what is to come.

Of course, I must admit my more selfish motives. I too need to pivot and to adapt to the unfolding revolution. A revolution in the way we do business internationally. I wrote this book to improve my own chances of survival.

I decided to approach this in a more formal way than I normally would. Like many, I have read extensively and I have tried to acknowledge this by naming those responsible for ideas that are not my own. What I have also done is spoken to people.

I have spoken to around 150 people in my network. Some are well known but most are not. What they all have in common is that they have done business across borders and in many cases, across several countries. They have also done so with some degree of success. I have captured a few of the interviews as videos on our website www.htj.tax but most spoke with me privately and I must therefore respect their privacy.

So where are we now? It is June 2020 and many nations are emerging from extreme social distancing policies or lockdowns. We are bruised, battered and scared. Scared of what awaits us.

It is my hope that this book helps you as it has helped me. My message? It's simple. You must diversify your lifestyle.

Happy reading.

Derren Joseph.
Connect with me on LinkedIn - http://uk.linkedin.com/pub/derren-joseph-ea/2/533/34

How to Use This Book

I assume that you already have a successful business. This book is not about growing your wealth. It is all about PROTECTING your wealth. It does this by introducing you to certain trends that I believe that you as an international entrepreneur should consider as you plan for this post pandemic world. We know how important it is to enjoy freedom while protecting your health and your wealth.

At the very start of the book, I get to the point. I share key factors that international entrepreneurs need to focus on in their strategic planning. The two most important factors entrepreneurs would to adopt in the post pandemic world would be

- A strong, high quality, residency and citizenship portfolio and
- A system for remotely managing your assets given the dynamics of the post pandemic world.

The rest of the book paints a picture of what lies ahead. Economic turmoil. Rising nationalism. Social unrest driven by rising inequality. Health concerns. Intrusive systems for tracking movement. But also innovation, creativity and an explosion of technology to take us forward. I hope that you see this book as sparking your curiosity around certain ideas rather than providing dogmatic answers.

My thesis is that this pandemic has created nothing new. Many would conveniently blame the pandemic but I hope that I demonstrate that the pandemic only accelerated pre-existing socio-economic trends and conditions. Use the Table of Contents as a guide, please jump directly to the Chapters that interest you.

It cannot be overemphasized that this book is not a replacement for getting proper international entrepreneur tax, legal and immigration advice. If our attorney had his way, we would print this in big bold letters on every page. We are international tax consultants, but we are not your international tax consultants. You need to have a team and you need to be in regular contact with them.

So, in this book, again, please use the Table of Contents and navigate to the sections you think of interest to you. Each chapter starts with "Take Away" so you know what that chapter offers and can consider if it's worth your time to read it.

I update my blog pretty frequently at - http://www.HTJ.tax

To provide feedback to me directly or to engage us, do connect with me and contact me on LinkedIn. I'm Derren Joseph - https://www.linkedin.com/in/derren-joseph-ea-0345332/

International Entrepreneurship in a Post Pandemic World

Chapter 1 - Post Pandemic Actions for International Entrepreneurs and Expats

Take Aways:

1. A cycle of lock-downs and re-openings may become the new norm

2. Countries allow their citizens to return but sometimes long term residents have been denied re-entry

3. Therefore a Plan B for residency and / or citizenship is now a must for international entrepreneurs

4. Typically the narrative around second citizenship / residency may have revolved around tax planning

5. The narrative will evolve to include health care systems, disaster preparedness, social stability, IT infrastructure (especially fast WiFi).

6. Those who can afford it, will continue to curate a portfolio of citizenship / residencies as they seek to avoid unrest, protect families and preserve wealth?

7. International travel will be forever changed. Expect to surrender more personal data and perhaps some type of "Immunity" or "health" passport

8. Should we be unable to access our onshore / #offshore assets due to travel restrictions, we need to ensure that we have power of attorney, logistics and IT structures in place to manage and access our assets

Review Your Portfolio of Citizenships and Residencies

In early March 2020, I was at home in Singapore as the pandemic began to worsen. In mid-March 2020, I left to visit nearby Indonesia for what I thought would be a few days. Before I could return, Singapore went into a more serious lockdown. As an Employment Pass holder for 7 years, I thought it would not be an issue as the procedure only required that we apply online to the Ministry of Manpower to get "permission" to return to Singapore.

At first I thought this to be a mere formality but my request was rejected and the email mentioned that Singapore was giving priority to taking care of Singaporeans. This was a wakeup call for me to review my residency portfolio. While waiting for 5 weeks in Indonesia, Singapore extended the lockdown several times. Then Indonesia itself decided to tighten its own lockdown and shut its airports after giving less than 12 hours' notice. So, I had no choice but to return to my home in the US unless I wanted to be trapped in Indonesia while their airport was shut. Of course, I am not alone as many of us found ourselves displaced during these lockdowns. I know dozens of people locked out of Singapore, Malaysia, Thailand and the Philippines because of a combination of government policies and flight cancellations.

Furthermore, when passing through Tokyo to return to the US in late April 2020, I recognised that some airlines / airports had a new protocol for deplaning passengers. It was no longer by class (First and Business Class normally deplane before Economy). Rather we deplaned by risk profile. Passengers that had been to China eg would exit separately from those who had not been to designated high risk destinations within the last 14 days.

Given that periodic lockdowns with short notice periods is the new norm, I realized it is now the right time to review my own residency portfolio. Up to this point, I considered three places my home. North Miami, London and Singapore. I need "First World" cities where I can work and connect with internationally minded entrepreneurs. Last year someone told me that Europe is about culture, America is about efficiency and Asia is about growth. An interesting perspective but I do enjoy spending time in and doing business in these three parts of the world.

Singapore is a low tax jurisdiction so it is my permanent base, but I need to count my days in the U.K. and the U.S. to limit my tax exposure there as these are (relatively) high tax jurisdictions for me. I realized that I needed another low tax base to act as a backup for when next I may be unable to access my home in Singapore.

Before continuing with my story, I want to first introduce the concept of Flag Theory to those who may be unfamiliar with it.

For those unfamiliar, I would suggest that you research the idea of Flag Theory. For me, it is about de-risking yourself by ensuring that you and your assets are not under the control of any single jurisdiction.

According to Wikipedia, Flag Theory is a term sometimes associated with a perpetual traveler. An idea which proposes that individuals live in such a way that they are not considered a legal resident of any of the countries in which they spend time or operate. Given the present political environment, I think not having a tax residence is a poor strategy.

However, I do advocate diversification whether to minimize governmental interference, or to maximize privacy. The basic theory proposes that each of the following should be in a separate country:
- Passport and citizenship – in a country that does not tax money earned outside the country or control actions.
- Legal residence – in a tax haven.
- Business base – where one earns one's money, ideally somewhere with low corporate tax rates.
- Asset haven - where one keeps one's money, ideally somewhere with low taxation of passive income and capital gains.
- Playgrounds - where one spends one's money, ideally somewhere with low consumption taxes.

Now taxes should not drive the strategy given the range of tax planning tools available. But it is one of many considerations.

Please note that there are companies that carry the name "Flag Theory" registered in various jurisdictions. Some offer services associated with this generic term.

I'm surprised that more people do not know about economic migration options which give you the ability to plant flags all over the world. If you run a successful business or have accumulated some wealth, very few countries do not have options for welcoming you. We deal most commonly with the U.S., the U.K. and countries in South East Asia such as the Philippines, Malaysia, Singapore and Indonesia but we work with established Migration consultants that offer the entire world.

I have since spoken with and read expert opinions from some of the more reputable migration consultants in my network. Please note that this is an area of professional practice infested with unscrupulous snake oil salesmen that act unethically and illegally. So, ensure that your chosen team is indeed an established team, officially recognised and experienced. Be warned!

Anyway, as I was saying before, Singapore is a low tax jurisdiction so it is my permanent base but I need to count my days in the U.K. and the U.S. to limit my tax exposure there as these are (relatively) high tax jurisdictions for me. I realised that I needed another low tax base to act as a backup for when next I may be unable to access my home in Singapore.

No one size fits all and for my personal preference for a tax efficient, "First World" city to act as a backup to Singapore, I chose Lisbon in Portugal.

Portugal as my Plan B

Portugal is accessible to me because I hold UK citizenship within my residency and citizenship portfolio. During this post Brexit transition period, under the terms of the Withdrawal Agreement, UK nationals and their family members arriving in Portugal before 31 December 2020 are still able to follow the procedure of registering as European Citizens, and enjoying full rights of residence in Portugal as though they would be at that point considered to be EU citizens.

After the transition period, the EU Certificate of Residence would be exchanged for a residence permit under what I understand would be softer rules than those available to non-EU citizens.

Under the EU freedom of movement rules, EU, Iceland, Liechtenstein, Norway and Swiss citizens have the right to establish residence in Portugal with no need for a permit. However, after securing accommodation in the country, they are required to:
- Within a maximum of 4 months, register with the Foreigners and Borders Service (SEF), which must be done in person at the local Town Hall (Câmara Municipal), who typically requires documentary proof of sufficient means of subsistence, so that the new resident does not become a burden for the State;
- Upon starting an employment or self-employment activity or, otherwise, no later than the end of the then calendar/tax year, register as tax residents with the Tax and Customs Authority (AT), which may be done at any Tax Office (Repartição de Finanças) or Citizen's Shop (Loja do Cidadão), where documentary evidence of a title to residential accommodation must be shown.

Once registered with SEF, in the event the new resident individual has dependent family members - spouse (or common law spouse of at least 3 years), dependent children or dependent parents - who are not entitled to the EU freedom of movement, they may then apply for residence cards, valid for 5 years.

The maximum absences from Portugal by the residency cardholder must not exceed the following periods:
- 6 consecutive months per year, with no need for justification; or
- 12 consecutive months for important reasons such as:
    - being pregnant or giving birth;
    - having a serious disease;
    - being enrolled for a course of studies or professional training;
    - being posted abroad for professional reasons;
- or a longer period for fulfilling military obligations.

After having the Residency Card for 5 years, it may be possible to apply for Portuguese citizenship after 5 years of holding legal residency (whether residency card or residence certificate), subject to passing a language test of "basic Portuguese". I speak passable Spanish so I do not think it will be a problem for me to learn basic Portuguese.

An individual becomes a tax resident of Portugal upon registering as such, for which he/she must have the right to reside in the country and title to a place of abode therein, there being no minimum stay requirements. On the other hand an individual will under applicable law be deemed Portugal tax resident if, among other circumstances, he/she:
- either spends more than 183 days in the country, whether or not consecutive, in any given 12-month period; or
- has a place of abode in the country under circumstances that may lead to the presumption that this is his/her usual home.

Regardless of status, from the effective starting date of residence, a Portugal tax resident individual is liable to Portuguese income tax on his/her worldwide income, which must be all declared in the annual tax return. In any case, a newly resident individual that meets the eligibility criteria is entitled to benefit from "non-habitual resident" (NHR) tax status, which grants important tax exemptions. I am applying for this status.

The Portuguese tax year is the calendar year and liability to tax as a resident in the first and last year in the country applies on a split year basis. Once granted, NHR status applies retroactively from the first day of residence.

Portugal's NHR regime allows a 10-year tax exemption on most non-Portugal-sourced types of income. For the avoidance of confusion, please note that the NHR programme is just a tax regime that new residents may benefit from and does not in any way involve the granting of residence rights.

The NHR regime is open to anyone that meets its eligibility criteria. The only such criteria are that the applicant:
1. Has the right to reside in Portugal (an EU/EEA/Swiss citizen or the holder of a residence permit);
2. Has not been a tax resident of the country during the previous 5 years (hence "non-habitual", not a particularly well-chosen name);
3. Has title to the use of a residential property in Portugal (by either buying, renting or borrowing it);
4. Registers as a Portugal tax resident declaring such residential property to be his/her home; and
5. Applies for NHR status, which is done online, on the tax office portal.

Once obtained, NHR status will not in principle be lost under any circumstances during its 10-year statutory period. Even if the holder suspends his/her Portugal tax residence during this period, he/she will automatically reacquire NHR status upon resuming such residence.

NHR status grants a new resident of Portugal a 10-year tax exemption on most non-Portugal-sourced types of income, whether or not they are taxed at source, and whether or not, under a double taxation agreement (DTA), tax at source is reduced (e.g. on dividends, interest or royalties) or even eliminated (e.g. on pension income derived from private sector employment).

As with everything in this book, this is just an outline and you should do your own research and retain your own tax and immigration consultants to advise you. Tax is a very nuanced area of law. For example there are different categories of income which may not benefit from NHR. On the other hand, foreign self-employment income may be tax exempt in Portugal but only to the extent that it can be taxed in the source country under an applicable DTA signed with Portugal, meaning that the latter will have to be reviewed before a tax opinion can be offered.

Always seek independent tax and immigration advice before taking up residency or citizenship anywhere. Our tax team offers this all the time for clients seeking to move within Asia or to the US. Do consider it an investment needed to avoid future problems.

Focus on quality jurisdictions for secondary residencies or citizenship. Not just tax mitigation.

On the internet, the narrative around economic citizenship and economic residency tends to favor tax savings, tax havens etc. Perhaps this is because many of the YouTube channels and blogs tend to be dominated by service providers that serve middle income clientele. In this section, I would prefer to focus on high net worth individuals (HNWI).

About [108,000 millionaires migrated countries in 2018](#), compared to 95,000 in 2017, according to a study by New World Wealth (NWW). The global market research group ranked the flow of millionaires into 12 countries by dividing the number of new millionaires by the total number of high-net-worth individuals already living in the country.

The top 4 destinations for HNWI are [Australia](#), the US, Canada, and Switzerland. As you can see, taxation is not as powerful a factor as many assume given that these countries have relatively high taxes. This is because HNWI can afford to retain tax teams to mitigate tax issues anyway. So to a large extent, it is not as important as other factors such as education opportunities for kids, safety and social life.

I remember seeing the New York Times, in February 2017. There was an article that said "The wealthy today don't have a country." It was a quote from Reaz H. Jafri, a New York-based partner at Withers Worldwide, a law firm that helps wealthy clients move and relocate around the world. "They don't view their success as being related or dependent on a single country, but on their own business strategies. It's amazing to me how many of the very wealthy are going totally mobile."

This accords with our experience as a practice. We have been with such clients for many years. But how does the pandemic impact this space?

Firstly I would anticipate an uptick in individuals securing second residencies and citizenship. When flights get grounded and lock-downs happen and it is not possible to access one's primary residence, it is helpful to have a second or third residence. I'm not just talking about residency documents but actual homes with clothing and all amenities. Remember in many cities, hotels were closed and visitors asked to leave.

Secondly, some jurisdictions responded less favorably than others in the pandemic. The weakness in health care systems was more evident in some jurisdictions than others. Furthermore, despite the availability of flights, some jurisdictions did not allow their own residents to return home. For example, in certain countries, being a long term resident was not enough to be allowed back in the country during the lockdown as citizens were prioritized. Thus alienating long term residents from their family, their businesses and their homes. HNWIs may wish to review their residency portfolios in light of such policies.

Thirdly, in speaking to citizenship experts while writing this book, I was told about rural areas within advanced economies. The US media has highlighted how Manhattan's elite practically evacuated the city and retreated to their country / seaside homes. For English speakers in cities with an international perspective, quiet parts of Europe and New Zealand have been particularly attractive. In a lock-down having a nice green estate around the home allows one to maintain social distancing without the cabin fever that comes with being in a confined space.

Be Prepared for Reduced Freedoms of Movement.

Given the desire of authorities to better track movement of both residents and visitors, one would expect that measures will be put in place. New systems to track who is infected and who isn't, and where they've been, have been created or extended in China, South Korea and Singapore. And a range of other surveillance systems – some utilizing GPS location data, some gathering medical data – have been debated or piloted in Israel, Germany, the U.K., Italy and elsewhere...including the US.

Whether the prospect on the table is "immunity passports" or cellphone-based tracking apps, the aim is to protect public health. But experts say it's also important to avoid a slippery-slope scenario where data collected to minimize the spread of disease is stored indefinitely, available without limits to law enforcement or susceptible to hackers.

Perhaps various jurisdictions will adopt different systems? Perhaps a uniform system will be adopted that involves a hybrid between a passport, bio-metric driven trusted traveler systems, and health data?

We can see harbingers of this in the measures some countries are taking today. Israel is going to [use the cell-phone location data](#) with which its intelligence services track terrorists to trace people who've been in touch with known carriers of the virus. Singapore does exhaustive [contact tracing](#) and publishes detailed data on each known case, all but identifying people by name.

We don't know exactly what this new future looks like, of course. But one can imagine a world in which, to get on a flight, perhaps you'll have to be signed up to a service that tracks your movements via your phone. The airline wouldn't be able to see where you'd gone, but it would get an alert if you'd been close to known infected people or disease hot spots. There'd be similar requirements at the entrance to large venues, government buildings, or public transport hubs.

There would be temperature scanners everywhere, and your workplace might demand you wear a monitor that tracks your temperature or other vital signs. Where nightclubs ask for proof of age, in future they might ask for proof of immunity—an identity card or some kind of digital verification via your phone, showing you've already recovered from or been vaccinated against the latest virus strains.

We'll adapt to and accept such measures, much as we've adapted to increasingly stringent airport security screenings in the wake of terrorist attacks. The intrusive surveillance will be considered a small price to pay for the basic freedom to be with other people.

As usual, however, the true cost will be borne by the poorest and weakest. People with less access to health care, or who live in more disease-prone areas, will now also be more frequently shut out of places and opportunities open to everyone else. Gig workers—from drivers to plumbers to freelance yoga instructors—will see their jobs become even more precarious.

In the meantime, it is no longer enough to have a "powerful" passport that allows visa free movement. It is necessary to be resident in (highly rated) cities that would not impede your ability to travel freely. Passport planning is no longer sufficient.

Acceleration of Remote Working and Learning

Take Aways:

1. Greater remote working and remote learning is one of the more obvious consequences of the pandemic

2. Like most of the other trends, it was on the upswing pre-pandemic but will accelerate post pandemic. Upwork's "Future Workforce Report" predicts that 73% of all teams will have remote workers by 2028 and 75% of current teleworkers say they plan to work remotely for the rest of their career

3. Technology tools like Zoom and Team plus stronger data security means that remote working / learning is here to stay

4. Remote learning is no longer an inferior option to in person classes. It has been legitimized

5. Rising remote work may disproportionately benefit higher income earners. Rising remote learning may disproportionately benefit lower income earners

6. In terms of real estate, it would of course vary by geography but generally speaking, it has been fundamentally impaired -

6.1 Retail space may continue to decline as shopping moves online

6.2 Industrial space will continue to grow as ecommerce requires up to three times as much warehouse space on average than traditional brick-and-mortar retailers

6.3 Office space may decline in some cities due to remote working plus economic contraction.

6.4 Coworking spaces / service offices with pre-existing problems (ie those that were unprofitable) will struggle

6.5 Residential may be impacted in some areas. In a February 2020 report from Zillow, more than half of home buyers who work remotely say remote work influenced a major home change, whether that's moving to a different house (28%) or to a different location (24%).

Perhaps the most obvious impact of the Pandemic is the push towards remote working. You MUST be able to run your businesses remotely. This is non negotiable. It is clearly not new but I wanted to go into it in more detail.

Some 74% of respondents in a 2018 survey in the US believe that flexible working has become the "new normal."

Working outside of their company's main location and having a choice of work environment is now a key factor for many job seekers when evaluating new career opportunities.

In the span of one year, from 2016 to 2017, remote work grew 7.9%. Over the last five years it grew 44% and over the previous 10 years it grew 91% in the US.

Between 2005 to 2017, there was a 159% increase in remote work. In 2015, 3.9 million U.S. workers were working remotely. Today that number is at 4.7 million, or 3.4% of the population.

What's driving this trend?
- Explosion of collaboration and productivity tech. Cloud-based technologies like Zoom, Slack, and JIRA are helping enable the communication — both synchronous and asynchronous, written and verbal — required to work remotely.
- Workers increasingly demand flexibility.
- Companies are global from day one. The Internet has opened the door for companies to hire talent all over the world, not just within close proximity of their offices.
- Workplaces optimizing for productivity not presence.

Remote Work Is More Prevalent in Certain Areas

However, do consider that remote work is and will continue to be more common with knowledge workers who are typically paid higher salaries, such as software engineering and marketing. Regardless, for those sectors where can be deployed, it widely believed that -

- Remote Work Attracts and Retains Talent
- Remote Work can be good for Productivity
- Remote Work Increases Job Satisfaction
- Remote Workers take fewer sick days
- Remote Work Is Environmentally Friendly given the reduction in commutes.

Despite the limited scope of remote working, Upwork's "Future Workforce Report" predicts that 73% of all teams will have remote workers by 2028 and 75% of current teleworkers say they plan to work remotely for the rest of their career

But there is nothing new here. We all knew this but there are serious economic implications as remote working and remote learning increases. Let us explore some of these.

Commercial Real Estate

Among the sectors impacted by remote working is real estate. Of course real estate markets vary widely depending on geography. But in many developed urban markets, there are those who would argue that real estate as an asset class is now fundamentally impaired due to technology. In the commercial sector, ecommerce will continue to shape the retail market for years. Before the pandemic, estimates were that 12.4 % of total US retail sales come from ecommerce, but that number is expected to grow significantly as ecommerce will shape the retail market.

Industrial real estate will thrive as with more online shopping, demand and pricing for warehouse space will surge. Estimates are that e-commerce requires up to three times as much warehouse space on average than traditional brick-and-mortar retailers with the average consumer product like toothpaste being stored in four or more distribution warehouses from point of manufacture to point of retail consumption. Additionally, as consumers' expectations accelerate to same-day fulfillment—and even one-hour delivery—many industrial tenants are sourcing smaller distribution sites in more densely populated locations. Not to mention the reverse logistics aspect of ecommerce as retailers need facilities to process returns which adds to overall demand.

Last-mile delivery that is close to the end user means they are constantly looking for space that is closer to the end user, so companies are increasing reliance on last-mile distribution centers near population centers. This last-mile focus is driving Amazon and other retailers to seek additional warehouse space near large cities to facilitate quicker and more efficient distribution to customers. It is estimated that Amazon already has centers located within 20 miles of half the population in the U.S.

But what about office space? When the Great Recession hit back in 2008, many US companies downsized their office space to save money and began allowing, or even encouraging, employees to work from home. What was born from necessity stuck around long after the economy rebounded. It is natural to expect the decline to continue in the post pandemic world.

Based on this trend, many have been betting on co-working spaces and serviced offices. Although people typically associate coworking with freelancers and startups, Fortune 500 and enterprise companies such as Salesforce, Microsoft, UBS, and others also utilize coworking spaces. It makes sense. They're essentially beautiful office space, plus amenities, plus community all included in a turnkey package.

Around mid-2019, global coworking giant WeWork boasted 425 locations in 100 cities as it headed for a buzzy IPO with a valuation of $47 billion filed in an S-1 by its larger-than-life cofounder and CEO, Adam Neumann. But then there was that little IPO failure. The one that made international news; resulted in the exit of Neumann (who jumped with a $1.7 billion parachute from his role as chairperson of the board); dominoed into layoffs of 2,400 employees by late November; and left lots and lots of not-so-glowing articles, blog posts, and industry distaste in its wake.

After WeWork's fall from grace, some have asked if coworking dead. In some geographies, it is definitely struggling but others are going strong.

Residential Real Estate

In a February 2020 report from Zillow, more than half of home buyers who work remotely say remote work influenced a major home change, whether that's moving to a different house (28%) or to a different location (24%).

Additionally, 30% of home buyers indicated that a commute between 15 and 29 minutes was their max. And only 12% of home buyers said they were willing to commute an hour or more.

Furthermore, 62% of Gen Z and millennial home buyers work remotely at least one day per week. Remote work gives the workforce's two youngest generations, who are often burdened with student debt, more options with where they live, reducing the necessity to live near large metropolitan city centers in order to maximize career potential.

So for urban spaces that are overly dependent on workers from sectors benefiting from remote work, it is not unreasonable to expect that certain residential developments would be impacted.

Learning and Development

Educational institutions across the globe have been impacted by the pandemic. In response, school administrators and teachers have been converting in-person curriculum into online courses.

Online education has seen exponential growth in recent years. From 2008 to 2017, the percentage of undergraduates enrolled in the U.S. in at least one distance education class expanded from 20-32% of all enrollments, according to the Institute of Education Sciences. Often students are the pioneers in new technology adoption, setting the pace for other vertical industries. Educational institutions have been an avid adopter of advanced synchronous and asynchronous communications for online learning. Rapid consumerization, the impact of social media, and the growing popularity of flipped classrooms and blended learning have led to the increasing use of technology in education.

Video conferencing-based remote learning keeps students engaged with features like whiteboarding, annotation, group chat, breakout rooms, attention tracking, etc. Many K-12 schools have been avid users of Google Classroom, the online platform that allows teachers to post videos and assignments.

Many universities are already leveraging video conferencing as a key part of their educational toolset. Arizona State University is one of the largest universities in the US. Like most American universities, they switched to remote teaching and in the second week of March 2020, held 170 classes with 7,000 students using Zoom. Similarly, the University of Bologna, Italy, which has an enrollment of over 80,000 students, switched 90% of its courses to online using Microsoft Teams to run virtual classes within 3-4 days after the Italian government closed the doors.

This isn't the first time that the video conferencing industry has seen a spike in demand. In years past, events such as Sept. 11 and the SARS outbreak have prompted businesses to use video meetings in lieu of travel. However, past surges failed to leave a lasting impact on the industry. Frost & Sullivan research shows that only 6% of all meeting rooms globally are video conferencing enabled. The scale of the disruptions caused by COVID-19, however, is truly unprecedented and is expected to fundamentally change user behavior towards remote work and online education.

Part of what makes this crisis different is the technology that is enabling the response. Previous generations of video conferencing technology were complex, clunky, and costly to operate. Modern video meetings are simple to deploy, easy to use, and affordable for businesses of all sizes. However, the stickiness this time goes beyond technology considerations and touches upon human nature – the one constant that impacts adoption more than any other factor.

In recent research, Frost & Sullivan has pointed at the growing future of work trends such as the rise in distributed, dynamic, and on-demand work enabled by next-gen cloud and software delivery. COVID-19 will accelerate the need for flexible and agile work styles and further push the adoption of technologies that improve work-life balance.

Rising Importance of Third-Party Professional Services such as Family Offices

Reduced freedom of movement amidst unpredictable cycles of lockdowns and re-openings has implications. It means that for the international entrepreneur or expat, there would be circumstances where they would be unable to physically access their financial institutions, brokers and physical storage facilities.

Yes there is online banking etc but I have had clients who, like myself, were on a quick business trip when an unexpected lockdown was quickly instituted by the state.
- They did not have their bank token as they left it at their primary home before travel.
- If a card is lost or stolen while overseas? Some financial institutions only deliver card replacements to the address on their records - not your hotel in a foreign country.
- If your phone is lost or stolen while abroad, how would you get a replacement sim card overseas when that specific number is tied to verification protocols for accessing financial institutions or even government portals.
- Wifi may be slow in your location which restricts access to certain online portals which presume fast wifi.
- If you use a precious metal storage facility and your store physical metals yourself instead of using a third party service provider. How do you get to the vault on your own during a lockdown?
- What about paying important bills to various government departments when you are physically locked out of the country without the relevant access to online portals. Remember some government websites restrict access from overseas IP addresses.
- What about international tax rules around economic substance, nexus and permanent establishment when Board Members or key corporate decision makers -
  - cannot make it to physical meetings where these are a requirement for maintaining substance or
  - Are locked down in certain jurisdictions but still manage and control their international companies and international investments?

Beyond issues of economic substance which have implications for corporate tax, what about other International Tax issues?

- International Entrepreneurs and Expats may unintentionally overstay and trigger the equivalent of Substantial Presence in the U.S. and other jurisdictions which may lead to additional Tax Liabilities.

- Overstaying may trigger a loss of tax benefits such as -
    - UK citizens who may overstay in the UK and trigger UK tax residence through the statutory residence test
    - U.S. citizens who lose the Foreign Earned Income Exclusion because they are required to remain on U.S. soil

You get the picture. These are circumstances that have personally happened to me or my clients so they are very real. If you are an international entrepreneur? You can think of many more yourself.

The only reliable plan involves retaining reliable third party professionals on retainer. Professionals who are already authorized, to manage resources on your behalf. This could be as simple as giving your accountant or attorney formal "power of attorney".

But for those with a larger portfolio of investments, increasingly a Family Office is seen as the sensible solution. A Family Office is a private wealth management advisory firm that serves ultra-high-net-worth (UHNW) investors. They are different from traditional wealth management shops in that they offer a total outsourced solution to manage the financial and investment side of an affluent individual or family.

For the rest of this chapter I will give those unfamiliar with the concept, a sense of the range of services that a Family Office can offer. I think the need for such a wide range of services is more important than ever. Feel free to skip to the next Chapter if you think this is not relevant to you.

Many family offices handle budgeting, insurance, charitable giving, family-owned businesses, wealth transfer, and tax services. In addition, the family office can also handle non-financial issues such as private schooling, travel arrangements, and miscellaneous other household arrangements such as paying bills.

Family offices are typically either defined as single family offices or multi-family offices – sometimes referred to as MFOs. Single family offices serve just one ultra-affluent family while multi-family offices are more closely related to traditional private wealth management practices, seeking to build their business upon serving many clients. Multifamily offices are more prevalent due to economies of scale that allow for cost sharing among the clientele.

The Many Disciplines of a 'Family Office'

For many, Family Offices are all about substance. Establishing that key decisions are being made by the Family Office so that there is no doubt as to where activities are being taxed.

For others, Family Offices are about providing professional advice and services for wealthy families under a comprehensive wealth management plan.

In many cases, this is far beyond the capacity of any one professional advisor. It requires a well-coordinated, collaborative effort by a team of professionals from the legal, insurance, investment, estate, business and tax disciplines to provide the scale of planning, advice and resources needed. Most family offices combine asset management, cash management, risk management, financial planning, lifestyle management and other services to provide each family with the essential elements for addressing the pivotal issues it faces as it navigates the complex world of wealth management.

Legacy Planning and Management

After a lifetime of accumulating wealth, high-net-worth families are confronted with several obstacles when trying to maximize their legacy, including confiscatory estate taxes, complex estate laws, and complicated family or business issues. A comprehensive wealth transfer plan must take into account all facets of the family's wealth including the transfer or management of business interests, the disposition of the estate, management of family trusts, philanthropic desires and continuity of family governance. Family education is an important aspect of a family office; this includes educating family members on financial matters and instilling the family values to minimize intergenerational conflicts. Family offices work collaboratively with a team of advisors from each of the necessary disciplines to ensure the family's wealth transfer plan is well-coordinated and optimized for its legacy desires.

Lifestyle Management

Many family offices furthermore act as a personal concierge for families, handling their personal affairs and catering to their lifestyle needs. This could include conducting background checks on personal and business staff; providing personal security for home and travel; aircraft and yacht management; travel planning and fulfillment; and streamlining business affairs.

Moving beyond 2020, both single- and multi-family offices will continue to expand their focus to include much more than just wealth management, legal and governance. Other main areas that will see a lot of attention include working toward real-time consolidated reporting, developing soft factors like defining a clear mission and purpose and negating new risks like the complex universe of cybersecurity.

In short, the combination of continued global uncertainty and new wealth sets the scene for sustained growth of the family office sector. As requirements become more complex and holistic, we can expect to see the family office offering evolve to include a renewed focus on those elements that will help build strong family brands and manage solid reputations.

Chapter 2 - Lessons from the Past

I am a huge fan of history. It is said that there is nothing new under the sun. Events occur in cycles and the advantage goes to those who spot trends and prepare accordingly. George Orwell also famously wrote that "Who controls the past controls the future: who controls the present controls the past." Let that sink in.

Now let's look at three recent outbreaks.

Lessons from 1918 Spanish Flu

Some tell me that it is way too early to grasp the economic impact of the present pandemic. But international entrepreneurs and expats do not have the luxury of remaining in "wait and see" mode. So a rough sense of outcomes is needed to help forward planning

The 1918 Flu Pandemic which lasted from January 1918 to December 1920, is estimated to have infected 500 million people, or one-third of the world's population. This led to around 50 million deaths worldwide, with 550,000-675,000 occurring in the United States. The pandemic thus killed about 0.66 percent of the U.S. population. But a key difference from the present pandemic is that Spanish Flu was fatal for young (18-44), healthy adults.

NPIs or Non-pharmaceutical interventions implemented in 1918 mirror many of the policies used today. They included closure of schools, theaters, churches, bans on public gatherings and funerals, quarantines of suspected cases, and restrictions on business hours.

Research published in April 2020 by the World Economic Forum makes two key if somewhat obvious points -

- First, areas that were more severely affected by the 1918 Flu Pandemic saw a sharp and persistent decline in real economic activity.
- Second, we find that cities that implemented early and extensive NPIs suffered no adverse economic effects over the medium term. On the contrary, cities that intervened earlier and more aggressively experienced a relative increase in real economic activity after the pandemic subsided.

As would be expected, severely affected areas experienced a relative decline in manufacturing employment, manufacturing output, bank assets, and durable goods consumption. Exposed areas also saw a rise in bank charge-offs, reflecting an increase in business and household defaults. These patterns are consistent with the notion that pandemics depress economic activity through reductions in both supply and demand. Importantly, the declines in all outcomes were persistent, and more affected areas remained depressed relative to less exposed areas from 1919 through 1923.

Comparing cities by the speed and aggressiveness of NPIs, early and forceful NPIs did not worsen the economic downturn. On the contrary, cities that intervened earlier and more aggressively experienced a relative increase in manufacturing employment, manufacturing output, and bank assets in 1919, after the end of the pandemic. Regression modeling suggest that the effects were economically sizable. So reacting ten days earlier to the arrival of the pandemic in a given city increased manufacturing employment by around 5 percent in the post-pandemic period. Likewise, implementing NPIs for an additional fifty days increased manufacturing employment by 6.5 percent after the pandemic.

Lessons from the 2002 SARS

In 2004, the Institute of Medicine hosted a Forum on Microbial Threats. Out of this workshop came a paper on the economic impact of the 2002 coronavirus outbreak. I reference that paper in this section. Their report summarized three mechanisms by which SARS influenced the global economy.

- First, fear of SARS infection led to a substantial decline in consumer demand, especially for travel and retail sales service. The fast speed of contagion made people avoid social interactions in affected regions. The adverse demand shock became more substantial in regions that had much larger service-related activities and higher population densities, such as Hong Kong or Beijing. The psychological shock also rippled around the world, because the world.

- Second, the uncertain features of the disease reduced confidence in the future of the affected economies.

- Third, SARS increased the costs of disease prevention, especially in the most affected industries such as the travel and retail sales service industries.

Consider that Asian economies were still struggling to recover from the region's 1997 financial crisis and the bursting of the dotcom bubble when SARS first struck in November 2002. The death of a farmer in Guangdong, China, from a mystery flu-like virus would be the catalyst for the third major economic event to strike the region, as the type of pneumonia he was carrying — later named Severe Acute Respiratory Syndrome (SARS) — quickly became a pandemic.

People started falling ill across several major Chinese cities, including Shanghai and Beijing. Within a few weeks, the virus had moved across borders, initially to Vietnam, Hong Kong, Taiwan and Singapore and then much further afield. Dozens of deaths were reported.

Suddenly, many normally bustling Asian cities were eerily quiet. Business districts and shopping malls emptied and tourism and corporate travel were postponed on a large scale in favor of teleconferencing.

Airports and ports used thermal imaging to screen travelers. People who had come into contact with suspected SARS cases were quarantined and those who reported flu-like symptoms were advised to stay home. Those that did venture out wore face masks, and taxis could only attract passengers if they drove with their windows open.

Hong Kong University professor YC Richard Wong co-authored a paper on the economic impact of SARS on the Chinese territory. He described how the financial hub had just begun to see signs of economic recovery when the virus struck.

"The outbreak of SARS hit Hong Kong at a very bad time," he wrote. "Domestic demand collapsed before it had an opportunity to recover. Local consumption and the export of services related to tourism and air travel were severely affected."

- China saw foreign tourism revenue fall as much as 60% in 2003, while Hong Kong saw the number of visitors drop by 60% at the height of the crisis. Singapore and South Korea witnessed 40% falls, and Thailand and Malaysia saw drops of more than a third.

- Hong Kong hotel occupancy rates fell from around 79% in early March to just 18% in May and the number of airline passengers carried to and from its international airport fell by more than three quarters during the pandemic.

- Thousands of regional flights were canceled due to a lack of demand — Taiwanese airlines alone grounded nearly 800 flights, or 23% of their normal schedule, at the peak of the outbreak. The territory's public transport network saw daily ridership drop by half during the same period.

- At the height of the SARS outbreak, China set up mobile fever clinics to screen local residents for the virus

- Across Asia, hotels, restaurants, cinemas and other entertainment venues struggled to attract enough trade to remain in business, and major events, including music concerts and conventions, were called off.

Economists have estimated that SARS was responsible for a 1-2% dent in China's economic growth, and 0.5% across Southeast Asia in 2013. One report for the Center for International Development said SARS caused a $25 billion (€22.5 billion) loss to China's economy alone. Another by researchers at Australia's Griffith University put the global impact at anywhere between $30 and $100 billion.

The economic burden in SARS' ground zero — the Chinese city of Guangzhou — was estimated to be RMB 11 billion ($1.6 billion, €1.44 billion). The knock-on effect was also felt by China's manufacturing sector as shipments from Guangdong province to Hong Kong fell by a third.

SARS exacerbated an already weak labor market, with many retail, food and beverage and tourism-related firms across Asia laying off staff. Taiwanese firms introduced a system of job sharing while Singapore's government offset some of the impact with a relief package worth S$230 million ($170 million, €153 million).

SARS was made worse by a huge Chinese cover-up. Health authorities initially failed to alert the World Health Organization to several other cases in Guangdong, which could have prevented the virus' spread and reduced widespread public alarm described by Griffith University researchers.

During the nine-month outbreak, more than 8,000 cases of SARS were confirmed and 775 people died — 648 of them in China and Hong Kong. Then, as quickly as it emerged, the pandemic, which had spread to a dozen countries was over.

Most Asian economies bounced back — consumer demand and tourism quickly returned. China, however, faced international pressure to improve its transparency, preparedness and response to outbreaks of infectious diseases.

Lessons from the 2009 H1N1 / Swine Flu Pandemic

Within the past one hundred years, four pandemics have resulted from the emergence of a novel influenza strain for which humans possessed little or no immunity:
- the H1N1 Spanish flu (1918),
- the H2N2 Asian flu (1957),
- the H3N2 Hong Kong flu (1968), and
- the H1N1 swine flu (2009).

For this section, I rely heavily on the December 2016 issue of the Journal of Pathogens. The article was titled - "Reviewing the History of Pandemic Influenza: Understanding Patterns of Emergence and Transmission" by Patrick R. Saunders-Hastings and Daniel Krewski

So on March 17, 2009, the first case of a novel H1N1 influenza virus infection, also known as swine flu, was documented in Mexico. It rapidly spread throughout Mexico and the US and was declared a full pandemic by the WHO on June 11, 2009. Swine flu circulated around the world in two waves until August 10, 2010, when the WHO officially declared the pandemic over.

It originated in North American pigs, but spread to a few California and Texas children, and exploded in Mexico in March of that year. Fortunately, the 2009 H1N1 strain was not especially lethal, but it did prove unusually contagious as it caused one of the largest pandemics in modern history.

It is estimated that 700 million to 1.4 billion people contracted the illness which resulted in 150,000 to 575,000 fatalities worldwide. Do bear in mind that in 2009, many governments could not test everybody for this specific flu strain, so they just assumed that 'flu-like' symptoms were H1N1 (Swine) Flu. Sounds somewhat to the situation in 2020.

There is no commonly accepted metric to quantify the economic impact. On the low end, the 2009 H1N1, aka swine flu, outbreak had an estimated economic impact of $55 billion. On the higher end of estimates, the 2009 H1N1 virus which is accepted as being relatively weak, is estimated to have wiped 0.5 to 1.5 per cent off global GDP.

The pandemic also caused societal disruption and a substantial economic burden, which was documented more comprehensively than for past influenza pandemics. However, the total global impact of the pandemic is not well understood. First, direct costs related to treatment, with respect to drugs, outpatient visits, and hospitalizations, were high. In Canada, total costs have been estimated at around CAD$2 billion, with the care of hospitalized patients alone estimated to be close to CAD$200 million, as the cost of hospitalization for each H1N1-infected patient averaged about $11,000. Emergency department visits are estimated to have resulted in costs of another $50 million.

Overall, estimates of economic losses range from 0.5%–1.5% of GDP in affected countries. Such calculations, however, tend to underestimate other, often longer-lasting impacts related infection prevention efforts, such as school closures, lost productivity from work absenteeism, shifts in consumer habits, and reduced tourism. For example, although reactive school closures were implemented in many countries due to the high transmission rate in children, associated costs are difficult to calculate, as such action also leads to work absenteeism and lost productivity.

One study of the impact of school closure on households in New York City found that, in 17% of households, at least one adult had to miss work because of the closures. Though estimates vary depending on the size of the affected population and duration of closure, school closures have been estimated to cost from tens to hundreds of millions of dollars. The pandemic also negatively affected global tourism, with airlines reporting losses in the tens of millions. It is difficult, however, to disentangle swine flu's role in this decline, as the global economic crisis of 2008 was occurring simultaneously.

The response to the 2009 H1N1 pandemic, particularly in North America and Europe, demonstrated a significantly improved level of preparedness relative to past pandemics. This was the result of emergency preparedness efforts catalyzed by the earlier SARS outbreak of 2002–2003 and persisting fears surrounding H5N1 avian flu. Containment efforts employed a combination of pharmaceutical and non-pharmaceutical interventions.

In the United Kingdom, for example, an aggressive containment campaign combined school closure and voluntary isolation with antiviral treatment for suspected cases and mass prophylaxis of potential contacts; these interventions helped control the outbreak until more information could be gathered. The swine flu pandemic also marked the first pandemic response combining both vaccination and antiviral use.

In Canada, though an H1N1 vaccine was not approved until about six weeks into the second wave, the largest mass immunization program in the nation's history was carried out, with the federal government investing $400 million to purchase fifty million doses of the vaccine. High priority groups were the first to receive vaccination, before it was expanded to all groups a few weeks later. Between one third and one half of the population was vaccinated over the remainder of the pandemic.

Vaccination coverage was lower in the United States (with state averages from 12.9% to 38.8%), and much of Europe, with the exception of Norway (45%) and Sweden (59%). Unfortunately, there was little use of antivirals before September 2009, though awareness campaigns targeting primary care providers increased their use to treat patients later in the pandemic.

Non-pharmaceutical measures applied in response to past pandemics were again widely implemented to help contain the pandemic. The most common among these were recommendations for hand hygiene and voluntary isolation of symptomatic individuals. Canada did not recommend school closures to mitigate the pandemic but did benefit from closures for summer break during the first wave; estimates from Alberta suggest this reduced transmission among children by at least 50%.

Other countries, including the United States, United Kingdom, and Australia, did recommend and implement school closures. While there is uncertainty regarding the effectiveness of these interventions, research suggests strong compliance with, and public acceptance of, these measures.

Another important concern was the observed strain on public health, hospital, and human resources during pandemic peaks. While health systems were generally able to accommodate surges in patient demand, it is likely that an even marginally more severe pandemic would have resulted in harmful service disruption and the need to turn patients away. This was, in part, due to the need for doctors to issue antiviral prescriptions, which has since been addressed by extending this authority to pharmacists.

Overall, the 2009 H1N1 pandemic was a mild, albeit costly, global virus.

Chapter 3 - Trends before the Pandemic

My thesis is that the pandemic of 2020 has not created anything new in terms of socioeconomic trends. Rather it only accelerated certain pre existing trends. In this Chapter, I highlight three trends that were in play, pre-pandemic. In the following Chapter, I will discuss how the pandemic may accelerate these three trends. I'll start with perhaps the most important of the three - inequality.

Income and Wealth Inequality

The importance of inequality as a social trend was made clear to me after being exposed to the work of the genius that is Thomas Piketty. He is arguably among the world's experts when it comes to social, income and wealth inequality. I highly recommend his books and his videos. He has written on it extensively and references the hard data collected is available in the World Inequality Database (WID.world). This project represents the combined effort of more than a hundred researchers in eighty countries around the world. It is currently the largest database available for the historical study of wealth and income inequality both within and between countries.

I was born in London in the 70s. Growing up in the 1980s, I always had a sense that we were in a period of incredible social change if not social upheaval. There was a transition from a period of plenty and prosperity to one of economic contraction.

As an adult, I have been able to validate what I felt as a teenager in the 1980s. Inequality has increased in nearly every region of the world since 1980, except in those countries that have always been highly inegalitarian. In a sense, what is happening is that regions that enjoyed a phase of rising equality between 1950 and 1980 are moving back toward the inegalitarian frontier, albeit with large variations from country to country.

Inequality collapsed between 1914 and 1945–1950 in all countries for which data are available, and second, that while inequality has indeed increased since 1980, the magnitude of the increase varies widely from country to country. For example, the trends of the United Kingdom are closest to that of the United States. Income inequality in Sweden remains the lowest on the continent; Germany and France fall between these two extremes.

In Europe, the share of the top decile (the 10 percent of the population with the highest incomes) amounted to about 50 percent of total income in Europe in the nineteenth and early twentieth centuries until the beginning of World War I. It then began a fall between 1914 and 1945, eventually stabilizing at around 30 percent of total income in 1945–1950, where it stayed until 1980. European income inequality, which was significantly higher than that of the United States until 1914, fell below US levels during the so-called Trente Glorieuses 1950–1980, a period of exceptionally high growth (especially in Europe and Japan) and historically low levels of inequality.

In addition, the revival of inequality since 1980 has been much stronger in the United States than in Europe so that in the late twentieth and early twenty-first centuries the United States has taken the lead—the reverse of the situation at the turn of the twentieth century.

As a tax professional, I have been of course interested in the role that taxation has played in this evolution.

TAXATION

Among the changes that contributed to the reduction of inequality in the twentieth century was the widespread emergence of a system of progressive taxation of both income and inherited wealth. In short, the highest incomes and largest fortunes were taxed more heavily than smaller ones.

- I was surprised to learn that it was the United States that led the way.
- The United Kingdom also turned to progressive taxation. Although the United Kingdom experienced much less destruction of wealth than either France or Germany between 1914 and 1945, it nevertheless chose (in calmer political circumstances than prevailed on the continent) to reject its highly inegalitarian past by imposing steeply progressive taxes on income and estates.

Many are shocked when I say that in the period 1932–1980, the top marginal income rate averaged 81 percent in the United States and 89 percent in the United Kingdom compared with "only" 58 percent in German and 60 percent in France. Note that these rates include only the income tax (and not other levies such as consumption taxes).

In the United States they include only the federal income tax and not state and/or local income taxes (which can add 5–10 percent on top of the federal tax). Despite the narrative coming from the Righ, the fact that top marginal rates remained above 80 percent for nearly half a century did not destroy capitalism in the United States.

Highly progressive taxation contributed to the reduction in inequality in the twentieth century.

Under President Regan, progressive taxation was undone in 1980s America. The drastic reduction of top tax rates was the signature issue of the "conservative revolution" waged by the Republican Party under Ronald Reagan in the United States and the Conservative Party under Margaret Thatcher in Britain in the late 1970s and early 1980s. This political and ideological shift had resonated also around the world.

Now, in the United States the top marginal federal income tax rate has fluctuated between 30 and 40 percent since the end of the 1980s. In the United Kingdom it has ranged from 40 to 45 percent. In both cases, the top rate between 1980 and 2020 has remained at roughly half that of the period 1932–1980.

On one hand, advocates propose that the fall in tax rates reflected the idea that top marginal rates had previously risen too high. The argument goes that the high top rates had destroyed the entrepreneurial spirit of British and American innovators, allowing the United States and United Kingdom to be overtaken by West European and Japanese competitors (a prominent campaign issue in both countries in the 1970s and 1980s).

On the other hand, defenders of high taxes argue that other factors explain why Germany, France, Sweden, and Japan caught up with the United States and United Kingdom in the period 1950–1980. Those countries had fallen seriously behind the leaders, especially the United States, and a growth spurt was all but inevitable. Growth was also spurred by institutional factors, including relatively ambitious (and egalitarian) social and educational policies adopted after World War II. These policies helped rivals catch up with the United States and surge ahead of the United Kingdom, where the educational system had been seriously neglected since the late nineteenth century.

Furthermore, productivity growth in the United States and United Kingdom was higher in the period 1950–1990 than in 1990–2020. This weakens the argument that higher marginal tax rates kills industry.

Data suggests that the move to a less progressive tax system in the 1980s played a part in the unprecedented growth of inequality in the United States and United Kingdom between 1980 and 2020. The share of national income going to the bottom half of the income distribution collapsed, contributing perhaps to the feeling on the part of the middle and lower classes that they had been abandoned in addition to fueling the rise of xenophobia and identity politics in both countries. These developments came to a head in 2016, with the British vote to leave the European Union (Brexit) and the election of Donald Trump.

Falling tax rates on the wealthy must been seen as working together with the freer circulation of capital and increasing use of international tax planning to accelerate the aforementioned inequality.

INCOME VS WEALTH INEQUALITY

Wealth refers to the stock of assets held by a person or household at a single point in time. These assets may include financial holdings and saving, but commonly also include the family home.

Income refers to money received by a person or household over some period of time. Income includes wages, salaries, and cash assistance from the government.

In some ways, wealth is more important for understanding social inequality because wealth generates income, so income inequality depends in part on wealth inequality.

As for the evolution of wealth inequality, it was always much greater than income inequality. The share of private property owned by the wealthiest 10 percent reached 90 percent in Europe on the eve of World War I before decreasing in the interwar and postwar years to 50–55 percent in the 1980s, at which time it began to rise again. In other words, when wealth inequality fell to its historic low, its level was still comparable to the highest observed levels of income inequality.

Two facts appear to be well established, however.
- First, the increased concentration of wealth in recent decades has been noticeably greater in the United States than in Europe.
- Second, despite the uncertainties, the level of wealth inequality in 2000–2020 appears to be somewhat less extreme than in Belle Époque Europe. In the United States the top decile share is 70–75 percent of all private property according to the latest data, which is obviously significant but still not as high as the 85–95 percent levels observed in France, Sweden, and the United Kingdom in the period 1900–1910. The top centile share in the United States in 2010–2020 is 40 percent, compared with 55–70 percent in France, Sweden, and the United Kingdom in 1900–1910.

Given the rapid pace of change, however, it is not out of the question that the share of wealth belonging to the least wealthy 90 percent of the population will continue to decrease in decades to come.

As for Europe, this collapse of the share of the wealthiest is all the more striking because there was no sign that such an evolution was possible before the outbreak of World War I. In all European countries for which we have adequate wealth data, the concentration of property was extremely high throughout the nineteenth century and until 1914, with a slight upward trend and, at the end, an accelerating rate of increase in the decades prior to World War I. The same is true for countries where we have income tax data that allow us to study the final decades of the nineteenth century: for example, Germany, in which from 1870 to 1914 we find a growing concentration of total income due to income derived from capital.

So here's the key point to consider. Is it possible that the decreasing concentration of wealth in the twentieth century was an aberration? And from the 1980s we began a return to the "status quo"? Something to consider.

Economic Nationalism

When someone says Economic Nationalism? We think of Donald Trump, Brexit, Marine Le Pen, Norbert Hoffer, Nigel Farage, Geert Wilders.

I am aware of the alleged role of technology companies in manipulating voter behavior. But I believe that these firms manipulated forces that already existed. Again, they did not create the factors - just manipulated the behavior of social media users. They fanned the flames - they did not necessarily start the fire.

In this section, I quote extensively from research done by Ronald F. Inglehart from the University of Michigan and Pippa Norris from Harvard University.

As explained in the previous chapter, income and wealth inequality is rising. Blame is often placed on the rise of the knowledge economy, technological automation, the collapse of manufacturing, global flows of labor, goods, peoples, and capital (especially the inflow of migrants and refugees), the erosion of organized labor, shrinking welfare safety-nets, and neo-liberal austerity policies.

Rising economic insecurity and social deprivation among the left-behinds has fueled popular resentment of the political classes. This situation is believed to have made the less secure strata of society – low-waged unskilled workers, the long-term unemployed, households dependent on shrinking social benefits, residents of public housing, single-parent families, and poorer white populations living in inner-city areas with concentrations of immigrants-- susceptible to the anti-establishment, nativist, and xenophobic scare-mongering exploited by populist movements, parties, and leaders, blaming 'Them' for stripping prosperity, job opportunities, and public services from 'Us'.

However, the data does not support the reductionist idea that social inequality drives economic nationalism. Data is mixed and inconsistent. Populist parties did receive significantly greater support among the less well-off (reporting difficulties in making ends meet) and among those with experience of unemployment, supporting the economic insecurity interpretation. But
- In terms of occupational class, populist voting was also strong among the petty bourgeoisie, not unskilled manual workers.
- Populists also received significantly less support (not more) among sectors dependent on social welfare benefits as their main source of household income and among those living in urban areas.

Therefore, we need to consider another related theory. The cultural backlash thesis suggests that the surge in votes for populist parties can be explained not as a purely economic phenomenon but in large part as a reaction against progressive cultural change. A large body of empirical evidence documents these developments. Sectors once culturally predominant in Western Europe or the U.S., may react angrily to the erosion of their privileges and status.

Research concludes that cultural values, combined with several social and demographic factors, provide the best explanation for voting support for populist parties. There are those who feel that they have become strangers from the predominant values in their own country, left behind by progressive tides of cultural change which they do not share.

The distinction drawn between economic inequality and cultural backlash theories may be somewhat artificial. Interactive processes may possibly link these factors. Changes in the workforce and social trends in globalized markets heighten economic insecurity. This in turn, stimulates a negative backlash among traditionalists towards cultural shifts. It may not be an either/or question, but one of relative emphasis with interactive effects.

Regardless, economic nationalism was observed across the world before the pandemic. It was also translating into government policies. In Asia, where I spent much of the last 7 years, anecdotal evidence suggests that visa policies from China down to Indonesia were becoming stricter therefore impacting the mobility of foreign talent from the West.

Slowing Global GDP growth. Focus on Asia

To write a chapter on Global GDP trends would be ambitious. Especially since I wanted to make a single simple point. The world economy was slowing before the pandemic. To make this point, I am instead focusing on South East Asia. An area where I have spent much of the past 7 years.

Today
- Asia accounts for 42 percent of global GDP in purchasing power parity;
- this number was expected to rise to more than 50 percent by 2040
- Its share of global consumption grew from 23 percent in 2000 to 28 percent in 2017, and was expected to increase to nearly 40 percent by 2040.
- Asian corporations now account for 43 percent of the world's largest 5,000 companies (G5000), contributing $19 trillion in revenue to the world economy every year.
- Asia was the destination for $1 of every $2 in new investment in the past decade;
- 43 percent of the world's top 5,000 firms by revenue are headquartered in the region.

Throughout much of 2019 there were indicators of an economic slowdown across Asia. Referencing a Bloomberg report from July 2019, it was reported that gross domestic product in export-reliant Singapore shrank an annualized 3.4% in the second quarter from the previous three months, the biggest decline since 2012. China trade figures showed exports fell 1.3% year on year to June 2019. Imports shrank 7.3%.

Like South Korea's economy -- which already contracted in the first quarter -- Singapore is often held up as a bellwether for global demand given its heavy reliance on foreign trade.

Factory activity was also shrinking in 2019 across Asia and talk of a technical recession was already in the air amidst continued U.S.-China trade tensions and a cooling technology boom (particularly in semiconductors).

By the end of 2019, the IMF was estimating that China's growth was expected to moderate to 6.1. In India, growth decelerated sharply in 2019. In the IMF was saying that the ASEAN-5 countries (Indonesia, Malaysia, Philippines, Singapore, and Thailand), had been losing momentum in the first half of 2019, due to weakening external demand.

Fast forward to January 2020, McKinsey published a report called Corporate Asia: A capital paradox. I will quote extensively from this report which is freely available online. In this report, McKinsey explains that the influx of capital to Asia has not resulted in higher economic profit. In fact, Asia accounts for half of the deterioration in global economic profits from $726 billion to an economic loss of $34 billion from 2005-07 to 2015-17.

Asian companies may be scaling rapidly as capital floods in, but firms have been unable to deploy this capital in a manner that has translated into economic profits. Although Asian firms outperform on growth in invested capital, they have underperformed when turning it into "economic profit," (EP) a measure of a firm's profit after the cost of capital is subtracted. Corporate Asia is also underperforming other regions on average returns.

Corporate Asia turned an EP of $152 billion into an economic loss of $207 billion. Indeed, Asia accounts for almost half the global decline in economic profit between 2005–07 and 2015–17. North American firms, by contrast, were largely able to sustain their economic profitability, achieving a total of $245 billion, similar to $276 billion ten years ago.

Globally, ROIC declined by 3.2 percentage points from 11.0 to 7.8 percent between 2005–07 and 2015–17. While in Asia, ROIC declined by 2.7 percentage points from 9.7 to 7.0 percent over the same period. The fall in the ROIC of Chinese firms was even more substantial at 4.6 percentage points, from 11.4 to 6.8 percent. For other Asian firms, ROIC declined by 1.7 percentage points, from 9.1 to 7.4 percent.

Behind the averages in Asia, there were some pockets of significant value creation in major countries and in varied sectors. But hopefully I have made the point. There was a slow down in Asia before the pandemic.

Similarly, at a global level, there were signs of slowing growth. In fact, many were actively anticipating a decline. Given the length of the bull run, they argued it was almost inevitable and pointed to signs that it was almost here.

Now here we are. The black swan event some feared has indeed pushed us over the edge.

Chapter 4 - Trends to Watch in The Post Pandemic World

Economic Responses

Before getting into the specific trends, it would be helpful if I first explain what the post pandemic world looks like. This section largely references Mark Blyth research. He is a William R. Rhodes '57 Professor of International Economics at Brown University. He is a co-author, with Eric Lonergan, of 2020 Angrynomics. I also reference Gideon Lichfield from MIT

Two competing epidemiological models currently guide and divide expert opinion on how best to respond to the novel coronavirus.

The first, from Imperial College London, scared the U.S. and British governments into instituting strict social-distancing measures. It predicted that if left unchecked, COVID-19, the disease caused by the virus, could kill over half a million people in the United Kingdom and 2.2 million in the United States—not counting the many additional deaths caused by the collapse of each country's health-care system.

The second model, developed by researchers at Oxford University, suggested that the virus had already infected as much as 40 percent of the British population but that most had shown mild or no symptoms. According to this model, COVID-19 would still cause many deaths, and it would still severely stress health-care systems. But because it predicted fewer critical cases to come, the Oxford model suggested that an indefinite lockdown might not be necessary.

The attractions of the Oxford model are obvious. But if political leaders plan based on the Oxford model and turn out to be living in a world described by the Imperial College London model, they will have made a bad situation much, much worse.

Similarly, high-stakes decisions must be made about how to protect national economies from the effects of COVID-19—decisions that can be predicted with another kind of model. Political economists use "growth models" to describe what countries do to promote growth under normal circumstances, but these models also indicate how countries are likely to respond in the event of a crisis, such as a deadly pandemic.

The United Kingdom's basic growth model, for example, is driven by finance, housing, and, above all, domestic consumption. When the British economy got hit by lockdown orders, taking measures to boost consumption—such as guaranteeing 80 percent of wages—was the necessary response.

By contrast, in Germany, which is essentially a giant export platform sucking in demand from elsewhere, the necessary response included instituting a shorter workweek and guaranteeing company balance sheets, but not supporting wages.

Political economists use "growth models" to describe what countries do to promote growth under normal circumstances, but these models also indicate how countries are likely to respond in the event of a crisis.

For the United States, the question of how best to shield the economy from the effects of the pandemic is more complicated. In growth model terms, the United States is a massive exporter of primary products, aircraft, weapons, oil, services, software, e-commerce, and finance—simply because its economy represents a quarter of global GDP. But most of what drives the U.S. economy is still domestic consumption, but the role that private-sector debt plays in the U.S. economy makes it difficult to respond to a crisis like this one. This reality is thrown into sharp relief when contrasting the U.S. growth model with those of other countries.

Trade-dependent growth models, such as those found in northern and western Europe, tend to have large welfare states that help mitigate the effects of economic shocks. In general, the more open a European country's economy is to international trade, the bigger the welfare state it constructs to act as a buffer in case trade shuts off. Large welfare states also allow their citizens to carry large amounts of debt, since they effectively insure them against periods of unemployment; the most indebted people in the world are not Americans but the Danes and the Dutch.

In contrast, countries with growth models of the Anglo-American variety, especially the United States, tend to have weaker states, lower taxes, and large financial sectors. They have highly flexible labor markets rather than large welfare states, which means they ultimately depend on wages to drive growth. Since those wages have been buying less and less over time, credit cards, student loans, and medical debts have become a standard part of U.S. household budgeting. When those household budgets shrink sharply, their debts are not compensated by the shock absorbers that countries such as the United Kingdom and Germany have in place.

When systems such as the American one are hit by shocks, they tend to bail out their financial systems to keep credit flowing and let the real economy absorb the blow through unemployment and austerity policies. During a global economic crisis, the United States has one major advantage over other countries: it prints the global reserve currency. Other countries need U.S. dollars because their banking systems lend in dollars even though they can't print them. During previous crises such as the 2008 financial crisis, sharp falls in global financial markets have been put right by Federal Reserve actions such as rate cuts and bond-buying programs.

The U.S. growth model works well as long as there is little unemployment, wages are being earned and spent, and credit is being recycled to cover the difference between wages and costs by consumers and companies. But when markets freeze and cannot price assets correctly (no one knows how much United Airlines stock is worth because they don't know when Americans will be flying "normally" again), the growth model collapses. Once that happens, it is hard to find a bottom. The Federal Reserve and Congress can try to put a floor on asset prices by bailing out companies, but there is no bottom for the broader crisis of consumption that occurs when a third of the labor market is laid off and the other two-thirds are locked at home for an extended period of time. In this world, bailing out capital and expecting labor to adjust through wage cuts and unemployment is simply impossible given the scale of the shutdown.

The U.S. growth model is built in such a way that it simply cannot shut down without inflicting catastrophic damage on itself. Because the model is designed to adjust through reduced wages and employment rather than increased welfare outlays, political leaders can contemplate temporary unemployment benefits for a banking-induced shock, but not semipermanent cash transfers (which is what the British are doing) and a near-total collapse in asset values.

The British solution is too politically toxic to be anything other than a short-term expedient in the American context. So, once it became clear that—at least according to the Imperial College London model—the epidemiologically correct response was to put the economy in hibernation for several months, U.S. leaders started looking for other solutions.

President Donald Trump and proponents in many states elected to simply "restart the economy." The direct cost of doing so, according to the Imperial College London model, could be the deaths of as many Americans. But the United States, with its 330 million people, 270 million handguns, 80 million hourly workers with no statutory sick pay, and 28 million medically uninsured, faces challenges quite unlike those in other advanced economies. Putting the economy in a freezer for six months or longer would destroy what's left of its social fabric along with its growth model.

The United States will temporarily bail out companies, partially support consumption, and abandon lockdowns.

The U.S. stock market may soar if the Oxford model turns out to be correct, but that will do nothing for the millions of hourly workers who have been laid off, the thousands of small businesses that have gone bankrupt, and the millions of extra infections that will result if the United States opens for business too early.

Pumping the Brakes - Periodic Lockdowns

Regardless of which of the two models is correct, we can reasonably predict what will happen within the next couple years. I say within the next couple years because beyond that time scale, we could have herd immunity either through vaccination or natural immunity. So let's stick with the next couple years.

It's now widely agreed that every country needs to "flatten the curve": impose [social distancing](#) to slow the spread of the virus so that the number of people sick at once doesn't cause the health-care system to collapse. That means the pandemic needs to last, at a low level, until either enough people have had Covid-19 to leave most immune or there's a vaccine.

Here is the harsh reality - as long as someone in the world has the virus, breakouts can and will keep recurring without stringent controls to contain them.

Solution? Reimpose extreme social distancing measures every time admissions to intensive care units (ICUs / ERs) start to spike, and relax them each time admissions fall.

What counts as "social distancing"? The researchers define it as "All households reduce contact outside household, school or workplace by 75%." That doesn't mean you get to go out with your friends once a week instead of four times. It means everyone does everything they can to minimize social contact, and overall, the number of contacts falls by 75%.

Under this model, the researchers conclude, social distancing and school closures would need to be in force some two-thirds of the time—roughly two months on and one month off—until a vaccine is available, which will take at least 18 months (if it [works at all](#)).

Surely there must be other solutions. Why not just build more ICUs and treat more people at once, for example?

Well, in the researchers' model, that didn't solve the problem. Without social distancing of the whole population, they found, even the best mitigation strategy—which means isolation or quarantine of the sick, the old, and those who have been exposed, plus school closures—would still lead to a surge of critically ill people eight times bigger than the US or UK system can cope with. (That's the lowest, blue curve in the graph below; the flat red line is the current number of ICU beds.) Even if you set factories to churn out beds and ventilators and all the other facilities and supplies, you'd still need far more nurses and doctors to take care of everyone.

In all scenarios without widespread social distancing, the number of Covid cases overwhelms the healthcare system.

How about imposing restrictions for just one batch of five months or so? No good—once measures are lifted, the pandemic breaks out all over again, only this time it's in winter, the worst time for overstretched health-care systems.

If full social distancing and other measures are imposed for five months, then lifted, the pandemic comes back.

And what if we decided to be brutal: set the threshold number of ICU admissions for triggering social distancing much higher, accepting that many more patients would die? Turns out it makes little difference. Even in the least restrictive of the Imperial College scenarios, we're shut in more than half the time.

So a staggered pattern of social distancing would save more lives than a one-and-done strategy and avoid overwhelming hospitals while allowing immunity to build in the population. There is work done to support this by researchers at the [Harvard T.H. Chan School of Public Health](#) and led by [Yonatan Grad](#), the Melvin J. and Geraldine L. Glimcher Assistant Professor of Immunology and Infectious Diseases, and [Marc Lipsitch](#), professor of epidemiology.

The research supports multiple "intermittent" social-distancing periods (ie lock downs) that ease up when cases fall to a certain level and then are reimposed when they rise past a key threshold. The exact numbers, the work showed, depend on whether COVID-19 is a seasonal ailment like the flu and common cold — also caused by a coronavirus — or whether it is equally transmissible year-round. As time passes and more of the population gains immunity, they said, the restrictive episodes could be shorter, with longer intervals between them.

The question is whether there is the political will for intermittent social distancing periods ....or intermittent lock downs. Presumably some countries will do it and some will not. We need to be prepared

Rising Inequality

Take Aways:

1. As we enter summer, politicians face a very very serious dilemma.

2. The economic downturn is disproportionately affecting lower income groups

3. Income inequality may rise within certain nations

4. Aside from worsening poverty, other potentially negative outcomes include, spikes in mental illness, suicides, domestic violence, crime, and malnutrition

5. Economic inequality may rise between advanced economies and emerging markets

Social Inequality within Nations

More companies are asking employees to do their jobs from home. Cities and states are ordering nonessential businesses to close. Microsoft, Google, and Zoom have made versions of their work from home software free. Telecommuting is becoming the new normal for many office workers.

These mandatory closures may permanently change our work patterns. Employers may find employees do not want (or need) to return to the office once closures end. But that arrangement is only realistic for white-collar workers. Management, professional, and administrative careers overwhelmingly can take their work out-of-office. For most occupations, remote is not an option.

Arts and entertainment, accommodation, and food service workers are all but barred from remote work. A stagehand cannot move scenery from their home office. A bartender cannot pour a drink over the phone. A hotel porter cannot move bags via video conference. These are some of society's most at-risk workers. The average hourly wage for leisure and hospitality workers is less than $15/hour, per the Bureau of Labor Statistics (BLS). Now, with mandatory closures, these wage earners find themselves without jobs.

In 2018, only 29% of workers could even consider working from home, BLS data shows. While over 47% of those with at least a bachelor's degree worked at home sometimes, only 9% of workers with a high school diploma as their highest education level did.

Remote work arguably widens economic inequality. As the pandemic forces these changes, employees that can work remotely will do so.

Although the bipartisan Families First Coronavirus Response Act (HR 6201) in the US would provide relief for some industries, the provisions for emergency paid leave won't apply to many blue collar workers.

Taking a global perspective however, as of the end of March 2020, the OECD estimates that 1.7 billion people have been asked to remain at home by their governments, whether through a full lock-down or similar measures. As people are required to self-isolate and minimise social contact, using the internet and online platforms has become the safest way to access necessary goods and services. It is therefore not surprising that "gig workers" – workers that digital platforms hire on a per-service ("gig") basis – have been identified as "key workers" in the fight against Covid-19, be it delivering household necessities or performing services, such as stocking shelves in supermarkets or caring for the elderly or disabled.

Gig workers have also been identified as the highest risk group as they cannot always maintain safe social distance from their customers. Gig workers often live hand to mouth, and they just cannot afford to take time off. Moreover, some workers have leases and other upfront payments that they have committed to make to the platforms they work for, and they are simply unable to hold off work until they raise what they owe. It is worth noting that the gig economy also relies on workers in developing countries where overall most workers are informal and very often lack certain social safety nets.

Staying at home is a luxury for many. Michael Burry, the doctor-turned-investor who famously bet against mortgage securities before the 2008 financial crisis, became very active on Twitter in 2020. His message was that lockdowns intended to contain the coronavirus pandemic are worse than the disease itself. Burry says that Government-directed shutdowns in the U.S., which led to millions of job losses and may trigger one of the country's deepest-ever economic contractions, aren't necessary to contain the epidemic and have disproportionately hurt low-income families and minorities.

Burry earned his M.D. at the Vanderbilt University School of Medicine, but decided to become a professional investor after making hugely profitable bets in the stock market. He shot to fame after his hedge fund's bearish mortgage wagers were chronicled in "The Big Short," an Oscar-winning movie based on the best-selling book by Michael Lewis.

"Universal stay-at-home is the most devastating economic force in modern history," Burry wrote in an email to Bloomberg News. "And it is man-made. It very suddenly reverses the gains of underprivileged groups, kills and creates drug addicts, beats and terrorizes women and children in violent now-jobless households, and more. It bleeds deep anguish and suicide."

Consider Singapore which many would agree is a relatively developed, service based economy. By the first week in April 2020, social distancing policies meant that 239 companies had gone into liquidation since during the Q1 2020, compared with 287 for all of 2019. Another 19,000 companies had ceased operations since January - that is more than 200 companies a day, on average. Many of them faced liquidation. Eighty percent of restaurants planned to lay off staff.

Companies with cash on their balance sheets and private-equity firms, which have mountains of committed investor cash, may start acquiring weaker ones. Around the world, small and medium-sized firms are particularly exposed. In America, a survey published on April 3rd by MetLife, an insurer, and the us Chamber of Commerce found that 54% of non-sole-proprietor firms with fewer than 500 employees were either closed or expected to close in coming weeks.

So in a way, the pandemic has and will disproportionately impact companies with "preexisting conditions". A high profile case may be Boeing or Air Asia. Boeing's aircraft was involved in high profile crashes in 2019 while Air Asia was having issues making lease payments in early 2020 before the extent of the pandemic was widely known. So for many companies, especially SMEs with limited scope for Government bailouts, would see the pandemic as the straw that broke the camel's back.

Socially, the longer the lockdown lasts, history shows, the worse such outcomes will be. A surge of unemployment in 1982 cut the life spans of Americans by a collective two to three million years, researchers found. During the last recession, from 2007-2009, the bleak job market helped spike suicide rates in the United States and Europe, claiming the lives of 10,000 more people than prior to the downturn. This time, such effects could be even deeper in the weeks, months and years ahead if, as many business and political leaders are warning, the economy crashes and unemployment skyrockets to historic levels.

Already, there are reports that isolation measures are triggering more domestic violence in some areas. Prolonged school closings are preventing special needs children from receiving treatment and could presage a rise in dropouts and delinquency. Public health centers will lose funding, causing a decline in their services and the health of their communities. A surge in unemployment to 20% – a forecast now common in Western economies – could cause an additional 20,000 suicides in Europe and the United States among those out of work or entering a near-empty job market.

None of this is to downplay the chilling death toll COVID-19 threatens, or to suggest governments shouldn't aggressively respond to the crisis.

The medical battle against COVID-19 is developing so rapidly that no one knows how it will play out or what the final casualty count will be. But researchers say history shows that responses to a deep and long economic shock, coupled with social distancing, will trigger health impacts of their own, over the short, mid and long term.

Inequality Between and Among Nations

Joerg Wuttke, president of the EU Chamber of Commerce in China, says that if there is one lesson people are drawing from the pandemic in this regard it is that "single source is out and diversification is in." In other words, companies do not just need suppliers outside China. They need to build out their choice of suppliers, even if doing so raises costs and reduces efficiency. Many expect to see new demand for production in Vietnam, Myanmar and elsewhere.

For some, the need to have more suppliers looks like an opportunity to promote possibilities at home. The government-owned Development Bank of Japan plans to subsidise relocation costs of companies that bring production facilities back to the country. Rich Lesser, the CEO of Boston Consulting Group (BCG), which advises big global firms, says that robotics and other new approaches to manufacturing make the case for moving factories closer to home more compelling, because they reduce the cost difference. Just as previous information technology was put to work underpinning the spread of supply chains, so today's can be used to shorten them—potentially making companies more responsive to local tastes.

What about inequality among countries? If wealthier economies struggle, poorer countries simply lack the capacity to cope with economic shocks of this magnitude. It would be therefore reasonable to expect that the divide between wealthy and poorer countries will continue to grow.

To explore this we return to research published by Thomas Piketty.

As we progress in the twenty-first century, research is being done to better understand the relative and paradoxical pauperization of the poorest nation states. Particularly in sub-Saharan Africa and South and Southeast Asia.

There has in general been a good deal of variation in the rate at which poor countries have closed the gap with rich countries since the 1970s. The China-India comparison is discussed at length in various studies. China not only grew faster than India but also generated less inequality, probably because it invested more in education, health, and necessary developmental infrastructure.

More generally, we have seen that economic development has historically always been closely associated with state building. The constitution of a legitimate government capable of mobilizing and allocating major resources while retaining the confidence of the majority is the fundamental prerequisite of successful development and the hardest to achieve.

In this context just like we established that inequality within Western nations increased in the post 1980 period, it has been shown that the poorest states in the world became poorer in the post 1970 period.

Let's look at ASEAN as an example of what the post pandemic inequality among nations would look like.

ASEAN as an Example

Let's pivot to ASEAN. In recent years, ASEAN countries have become much more trade dependent on China. The volume of ASEAN-China trade stood at 345 billion dollars in 2015, the second largest after the 543 billion-dollar volume of intra-ASEAN trade. After China came ASEAN's trade with Japan, the European Union and the United States, with trade volumes of more than 200 billion dollars. China has been ASEAN's largest trading partner since 2009.

From 2005 to 2015, China's trade with ASEAN grew by the largest margin (13.2%) among its trade partners. South Korea-ASEAN trade grew by 10.9% over the same period, but ASEAN's trade with the EU, Japan and the US grew only by 5.4%, 5% and 3.6% respectively.

Pre-pandemic, China was slowing as explained in a previous Chapter. In August 2019, China saw industrial output grow at its slowest pace since 2002. Weeks later China's Premier Li Keqiang said it would not be easy for the country to sustain growth rates of above 6%. Domestic issues, the US-led trade war, and swine fever were already putting a brake on China's rapid expansion. Now we factor in the 2020 pandemic.

One would expect that a continued slowdown in China would adversely impact ASEAN. Sectors such as tourism, real estate and commodities would be severely impacted thus increasing the gap between wealthier and poorer nations.

Recent forecasts from the World Bank, the Asian Development Bank (ADB), and the IMF all see sharp declines in regional growth as a result of the economic shock of this pandemic, but they offer a range of projected growth. The ADB's Asian Development Outlook, which was released earlier in April 2020, forecasts that Southeast Asia will track closely with China and decelerate growth to +1 percent in 2020. The World Bank report, released in the beginning of April, includes both a baseline and a more pessimistic scenario, with the "lower-case" forecast projecting contractions of the major developing ASEAN countries in the -0.5 percent to -5.0 percent range, with the exception of Vietnam, which maintains positive (+1.5 percent) growth.

Although they measure a slightly different group of countries, the worsening of economic conditions and the ongoing spread of the crisis has lowered forecasts by these international financial institutions (IFIs) over the course of just a few weeks. Many private forecasts paint an even bleaker picture for ASEAN growth, projecting growth in the range of -1.5 percent for 2020.

Despite the increasingly pessimistic forecasts for the region, both the IMF and ADB project a strong rebound in 2021. The IMF projects growth for the ASEAN-5 to bounce back to +7.8 percent in 2021, while the ADB sees growth for Southeast Asia rebounding to +4.7 percent next year. In short, they see the global economic crisis brought on by the Covid-19 pandemic as a huge but relatively short-term shock. Only the "lower-case" scenario of the World Bank foresees a slower recovery, with the major ASEAN economies still in negative growth territory in 2021, again with the exception of Vietnam.

Country-specific impacts will depend on the structure of each economy and their initial economic conditions heading into the crisis. Hardest hit will be Thailand, which was already struggling in 2019 and early 2020 with a severe drought, budget delays, and a strong currency and was somewhat slow to respond to the onset of the pandemic.

The closely entwined economies of Malaysia and Singapore are forecast by the ADB to see close to 0 percent economic growth this year, with only Malaysia expected to rebound strongly next year. However, the IMF projects recessions for both economies in 2020, with Singapore projected at -3.5 percent growth and Malaysia at -1.7 percent. Singapore's own projections by its Ministry of International Trade and Industry have been revised down to between -0.5 percent and -4 percent growth this year, with the lower end more likely.

Indonesia and the Philippines are forecast to see sharp deceleration of growth, with the IMF projecting growth in the barely positive range. Vietnam stands out in all these forecasts as the only ASEAN economy to maintain moderate growth in 2020, in the range of +2.7 percent (IMF) to +4.8 percent (ADB), and is expected to strongly rebound in 2021 (+6.8 percent to +7.0 percent growth).

The impact of the Covid-19 crisis is hitting these economies through several channels.

First, ASEAN countries are highly open to trade and investment as well as tourism, all of which have been severely disrupted by the spreading global pandemic. Demand for these countries' exports—whether palm oil and metals from Indonesia; manufactured components from Malaysia, Vietnam, and the Philippines; or textiles from Cambodia—have fallen sharply and will continue to stagnate throughout the crisis.

The suspension and likely very slow resumption of tourism will hit the Thai economy especially hard, which depends on tourism and travel spending for one-fifth of its GDP, and will also impact the tourism-dependent economies of Malaysia, Indonesia, Philippines, and Vietnam. Singapore had already been hit by declining trade volumes in the midst of U.S.-China trade conflict in 2019 and is now facing a further drop in trade in goods as well as declining services trade and tourism.

ASEAN economies have a diversified set of trade and investment partners, including the United States, European Union, China, and intra-ASEAN trade. In normal times, this diversified portfolio of partners would provide a buffer for a regional economic downturn, but in this global pandemic all of these partners are facing a halt to or dimming prospects for growth.

Second, the collapse in oil prices caused by the sudden drop in energy consumption due to the widespread lockdowns and travel bans will have a sharp impact on economies dependent on exports of fuel, namely Indonesia, where coal and oil comprise nearly one-quarter of exports; Malaysia, where oil and gas make up about 16 percent of exports; and of course Brunei, whose economy is almost entirely supported by exports of crude and natural gas (over 90 percent of exports).

Third, the sharp drop in domestic demand due to lockdowns and other public health measures will have large multiplier effects on these economies, since consumption represents about 60 percent of GDP in the major ASEAN economies, with Singapore being an exception.

The fourth channel of economic impact from the global Covid-19 crisis is capital outflows. Whereas foreign direct investment is generally sticky, international portfolio investors in emerging market equities and bonds have driven large capital outflows as they seek safe havens in the face of the deepening global pandemic. According to the Institute of International Finance, capital outflows from emerging markets have totaled nearly $100 billion so far this year, with Southeast Asian economies taking a sizeable hit. Indonesia has seen an outflow of $8.2 billion in capital by the end of March. These outflows have led to regional currency depreciations, especially the Indonesian rupiah, which has depreciated 14.5 percent year to date, while the Thai baht, Malaysian ringgit, and Singapore dollar all depreciated by more than 4 percent in the March 2-19 period. Central banks in the region have also intervened to support their currencies, but tightening financial conditions complicate their efforts to maintain accommodative monetary policy and shore up their economies in the face of the Covid-19 crisis.

Over the longer term, it is difficult to predict the ultimate economic impact on Southeast Asia because there is vast uncertainty about how the pandemic will play out. It is likely to intensify the ongoing process of reshoring capacity away from China and the rest of East Asia. Although certain sectors in some Southeast Asian economies have benefited from recent supply chain shifts out of China, it is less clear that post-pandemic trends will be as favorable. National security considerations in the United States and other advanced economies now loom large over questions about pharmaceutical ingredients and inputs for and production of medical supplies, while travel disruptions and difficulties in the form of quarantines, health certificates, and fear of travel will likely further accelerate the shortening of supply chains.

The shift of economic activity to the cloud and the need for mobile tracking and other tech solutions to contain and respond to future outbreaks of the virus could benefit Southeast Asia, in particular countries like Singapore, Indonesia, and Vietnam, which are already on the leading edge of the mobile-app-based digital economy. A global or regional shift in demand toward digital applications, and government policies designed to support this sector, could spur innovation and boost entrepreneurs working on the digital economy, which would brighten the growth and development prospects for Southeast Asian economies once we get to the other side of this global crisis.

But is Inequality a Bad Thing?

On one hand, observers often say that worsening inequality stands as the source of social instability, the shift to the right and a backlash against (so called) globalization.

On the other hand, one can argue that inequality has actually stimulated innovation and growth for the benefit of all, especially in China, where the poverty rate has decreased dramatically.

But to what extent is this argument correct?

A similar argument could be made about India, Europe, and the United States—namely, that equality had gone too far in the period 1950–1980 and had to be curtailed for the sake of the poor. However, growth rates in both Europe and the United States were higher, in the egalitarian period (1950–1980) than in the subsequent phase of rising inequality.

The gap between top fortunes and the rest continued to grow even in the decade after the financial crisis of 2008 at virtually the same rate as in the two previous decades, which suggests that we may not yet have seen the end of a massive change in the structure of the world's wealth.

Every human society must justify its inequalities. In today's societies, these narratives comprise themes of property, entrepreneurship, and meritocracy. Social Darwinism means that wealth flows to the most enterprising, deserving, and useful. We discuss entrepreneurship next.

Entrepreneurship is dead. Long live entrepreneurship

Now let's explore the narrative around entrepreneurship.

Take Aways

1. There is no doubt that in the last couple decades, labeling oneself an "entrepreneur" has become "a thing".

2. Cheap debt and easy funding has indeed made it possible for "entrepreneurs" to create "pre revenue" businesses. Controversially, we have seen businesses with no clear plans for making a profit enjoy billion-dollar valuations.

3. The U.S. startup rate has been falling for decades. There are many reasons for the decline including demographics.

4. The narrative around "entrepreneurship" forgets that valuable companies take decades to build. Funds have been chasing negative-gross-margin businesses that grow really quickly. Think WeWork.

5. Postpandemic, will we see the air disappear from this bizarre Ponzi balloon created by the venture capital industry?

There is no doubt that in the last couple decades, labeling oneself an "entrepreneur" has become "a thing". Indeed, as mentioned in the previous sections, the myth around entrepreneurship has been used as a justification for the increasing social, income and wealth inequality explained in previous sections.

Waves of quantitative easing, cheap debt and easy funding has indeed made it possible for "entrepreneurs" to create "pre revenue" businesses. Controversially, we have seen businesses with no clear plans for making a profit enjoy billion-dollar valuations.

My thesis in writing this book is that the Pandemic did not create anything new in the world of business. It only accelerated preexisting trends. I want to point out that the U.S. startup rate has been falling for decades. The Kauffman Foundation, citing its own research and drawing on U.S. Census data, concluded that the number of companies less than a year old had declined as a share of all businesses by nearly 44 percent between 1978 and 2012. And those declines swept across industries, including tech. Meanwhile, the Brookings Institution, also using Census data, established that the number of new businesses is down across the country and that more businesses are dying than are being born.

There are many reasons for the decline including demographics. However, I want to highlight one of the dysfunctions within the entrepreneurship narrative by focusing on the technology sector. "Scale" "Hacks" and "fast growth" have become the name of the game. Part of this is the risk aversion of the financiers, who themselves want to have short-term wins and want to fund things that look like they're working in the short term.

But the problem with things that work really quickly is that they can stop working equally as quickly. In the narrative around "entrepreneurship", the ecosystem seems to ignore that valuable companies take decades to build. Funds have been chasing negative-gross-margin businesses that grow really quickly. Think WeWork.

Chamath Palihapitiya has pointed out that tech startups spend almost 40 cents of every VC dollar on Google, Facebook, and Amazon. I will now quote extensively from the 2018 Annual Letter from Chamath Palihapitiya's Social Capital.

We don't necessarily know which channels tech startups will choose or the particularities of how they will spend money on user acquisition, but we do know more or less what's going to happen. Advertising spend in tech has become an arms race: fresh tactics go stale in months, and customer acquisition costs keep rising. Ad impressions and click-throughs get bid up to outrageous prices by startups flush with venture money, and prospective users demand more and more subsidized products to gain their initial attention.

Warren Buffett once observed that this kind of arms race is not unlike a parade where one spectator, determined to get a better view, stands on their tiptoes. It works well initially until everyone else does the same. Then, the taxing effort of standing on your toes becomes table stakes to be able to see anything at all. Now, not only is any advantage squandered, but we're all worse off than we were when we first started. Such is the world of user acquisition in tech today: as growth becomes increasingly expensive, somebody must be footing the bill for all of this wasteful spending. But whom?

It's not who you think, and the dynamics we've entered is, in many ways, creating a dangerous, high stakes Ponzi scheme. Over the past decade, a subtle and sophisticated game has emerged between VCs, LPs, founders, and employees. Someone has to pay for the outrageous costs of the growth described above. Will it be VCs? Likely not. They get paid to allocate other people's (LPs) money, and they are smart enough to transfer the risk. For example, VCs habitually invest in one another's companies during later rounds, bidding up rounds to valuations that allow for generous markups on their funds' performance. These markups, and the paper returns that they suggest, allow VCs to raise subsequent, larger funds, and to enjoy the management fees that those funds generate.

Picture this scenario: if you're a VC with a $200 million dollar fund, you're able to draw $4 million each year in fees. (Typical venture funds pay out 2 percent per year in management fee plus 20 percent of earned profit in carried interest, commonly called "two and twenty"). Most funds, however, never return enough profit for their managers to see a dime of carried interest. Instead, the management fees are how they get paid. If you're able to show marked up paper returns and then parlay those returns into a newer, larger fund - say, $500 million - you'll now have a fresh $10 million a year to use as you see fit. So even if paying or marking up sky-high valuations will make it less likely that a fund manager will ever see their share of earned profit, it makes it more likely they'll get to raise larger funds - and earn enormous management fees. There's some deep misalignment here...

There's an analogy to be made between today's venture backed startup ecosystem and the American healthcare industry. Part of the reason why American healthcare is so expensive is because insurers, who play a key middleman role in setting prices for medical care, have a fantastic two-sided business model. High prices, which ought to be a cost of doing business for them, are actually a key revenue driver. Why is this? High costs allow them to charge higher premiums, allowing them to pull steadily more and more money out of patients' and payers' pockets. As a result, the cost of medicine steadily rises, as do the insurers' take. In the end, both patients and payers are the ones who end up as bag holders footing the bill. The same thing is happening in today's venture world. Highly marked up valuations, which should be a cost for VCs, have in fact become their key revenue driver. It lets them raise new funds and keep drawing fees. And just as insurers' business model translates into higher costs of patient care, so does the modern venture model translate into higher costs of, well, just about everything. We have higher salaries, higher rents, higher customer acquisition costs, Kind bars, and kombucha on tap! So if it's not VCs, who ends up holding the bag?

It's still not who you'd necessarily expect. Later-stage funds, who invest large follow-on rounds into these marked up companies, do indeed pay inflated prices - but they also usually get their money out first upon a liquidity event, and are also happy to exist in "Fee-landia". In some cases, high prices may even work to their advantage. They're able to hold certain late-stage companies hostage to their high valuations by demanding aggressive deal structures in return for granting "Unicorn Status" (the billion-dollar valuation that VCs so crave). Unlike in other pass-the-buck schemes, the bill is not getting passed from early investors to later investors. The real bill ends up getting shuffled out of sight to two other groups.

The first, as you might guess, are early stage funds' limited partners, particularly the future limited partners that invest into the next fund. Their money, after all, is what pays the VC's newly trumped up management fee: marking up Fund IV in order to raise money for more management fees out of Fund V, and so on, is so effective because fundraising can happen much faster than the long and difficult job of actually building a business and creating real enterprise value. It might take seven to ten years to build a company, but raising the next fund happens in two or three years.

The second group of people left holding the bag is far more tragic: the employees at startups. The trend in Silicon Valley today is for a large percentage of employee compensation to be given out in the form of stock options or restricted stock units. Although originally helpful as a way to incentivize and reward employees for working hard for an uncertain outcome, in a world where startup valuations are massively inflated, employees are granted stock options at similarly inflated strike prices. Overall, you can understand how this arrangement endures: VCs bid up and mark up each other's portfolio company valuations today, justifying high prices by pointing to today's user growth and tomorrow's network effects. Those companies then go spend that money on even more user growth, often in zero-sum competition with one another. Today's limited partners are fine with the exercise in the short run, as it gives them the markups and projected returns that they need to keep their own bosses happy.

Ultimately, the bill gets handed to current and future LPs (many years down the road), and startup employees (who lack the means to do anything about the problem other than leave for a new company, and acquire a 'portfolio' of options.) What is the antidote here? The antidote is two-fold.

First, we need to return to the roots of venture investing. The real expense in a startup shouldn't be their bill from Big Tech but, rather, the cost of real innovation and R&D.

The second is to break away from the multilevel marketing scheme that the VC-LP-user growth game has become. At Social Capital, we did this by actively shifting away from funds and LPs to rely only on our own permanent capital moving forward. Are we crazy to reject tens of millions of dollars a year in fees? We think not, and we believe it's time to wait patiently as the air is slowly let out of this bizarre Ponzi balloon created by the venture capital industry. In the meantime, we find comfort in the teaching of Andy Grove that only the paranoid survive.

----------------------end of extract from the 2018 Annual Letter from Chamath Palihapitiya's Social Capital.

Entrepreneurship will not disappear of course. But it is hoped that post pandemic, a more conservative narrative will be infused into the ecosystem.

Rising Economic Nationalism and Conscious Uncoupling

In the previous section on growing inequality within ASEAN, I mentioned the decoupling from China. Let's explore this in more detail.

Take Aways

1. The current crisis has shown that the world's dependence on global supply chains is a weak link

2. Going forward, companies may accelerate their supply-chain transition from China to other parts of Asia.

3. Europe and the US. will continue to protect strategically-important companies from overseas takeovers.

4. Even if a foreign policy "traditionalist" such as former Vice President Joseph Biden wins the November presidential election, resistance from Congress and the public will prevent the full-scale return of an expansive U.S. role in the world.

5. No other country, not China or anyone else, has both the desire and the ability to fill the void the United States has created.

Unfortunately, policy decisions around handling the pandemic have led to allegations of various government's hoarding medical equipment, pharmaceuticals, dollar liquidity, local markets, opportunities for exports, even aid to poorer countries. No I am not just talking about the US, but also Brazil, Hungary, India, the Philippines, Poland, and the UK.

While fear-based hoarding on a national basis is human and understandable, history suggests that it is counter-productive and costly as we learned in the early part of the twentieth century in the run up to World War II.

Both public health and macroeconomics demonstrated long ago that if every national government, let alone every household, tries to self-insure in a panic, the outcome makes everyone worse off. On the economic side, demand collapses, as do asset prices; liquidity and credit disappear; and shortages of critical components, skilled labour, and supplies of, yes, food and medicine emerge. Over time, those countries which try to be self-sufficient across the board and decoupled from the global economy just will end up suffering more from lack of diversified sourcing and unavoidable local shocks, though this harsh reality gets obscured in the current crisis.

Supply Chains

But looking beyond the pandemic. The current crisis has shown that the world's dependence on global supply chains is a weak link, especially for commodities with a concentration around what now seem to be vulnerable nodes. China, for example, accounts for about 50 to 70 percent of global demand for copper, iron ore, metallurgical coal, and nickel.

We could see a massive restructuring of supply chains: production and sourcing may move closer to end users, and companies could localize or regionalize their supply chains. This change is likely to become especially prominent in Asia, where a growing middle class creates its own demand for production. Intraregional trade, which has already driven Asian trade for the past decade, accounts for almost as much of the total in Asia as in Europe.

Going forward, companies may accelerate their supply-chain transition from China to other parts of Asia. According to a 2019 American Chamber of Commerce (AmCham) survey, about 17 percent of companies have considered or actively relocated their supply chains away from China. In some sectors. such as textiles, this has already been happening, and the supply-side impact of the coronavirus could accelerate this change.

- Japan's automakers and South Korea's electronics players have indicated that they may accelerate the diversification of the manufacturing footprint beyond China.

- France's Finance Minister Bruno Le Maire called on retailers to be "economically patriotic" and favor products from French farmers.

- Supermarket chain Carrefour said it would stop selling fruit and vegetables of foreign origin when there is a French alternative.

- In Italy, Minister of Foreign Affairs Luigi Di Maio appealed to the population of the worst-hit country to "Buy Italian."

- In Portugal, where the economy minister asked the population to buy domestic products, as reported by the Lisbon newspaper Público.

- Belgian Finance Minister Alexander De Croo has warned of intra-European moves towards economic nationalism.

Impact on Foreign Direct Investment (FDI)

There is potential for the pandemic to trigger a downturn in flows likely made more acute by increasing efforts to control FDI in two of its main destinations, Europe and the US. This is to protect strategically-important companies from overseas takeovers.

Beijing's position as a major provider and recipient of FDI is expected to be affected significantly by the pandemic, which may increase developed world nervousness over predatory Chinese investment and China's value as a major manufacturing hub.

A worldwide FDI recovery will clearly depend on the efficacy of governmental crisis-mitigation measures, in tackling the spread of the virus and supporting business. But when that recovery comes, the foreign investment landscape may have changed markedly.

In late March the UN trade, development and investment agency, UNCTAD, forecast that the pandemic could cause global FDI to fall by up to 40% this year through to next. The announcement came a day after Europe expressed heightened concern about the vulnerability of companies to acquisition by foreign investors, as share prices tumble, with EU member states called upon to step up screening of inward investment.

The UN forecast for FDI falls, more than double an estimate in early March, assessed that the pandemic, coupled with government lockdown measures, would put severe pressure on FDI worldwide, with the worst-hit sectors including energy-related industries, airlines and car-manufacturing.

According to the UN, the closure of businesses, manufacturing plants and construction sites is causing immediate delays in the implementation of investment projects; while completions of merger and acquisitions are running into delays that could result in cancellations. It reported a large slump in the number of such deals in recent months, from an average of 1,200 a month last year to 385 in March.

Rising labour costs in China and the punitive tariffs imposed in the trade war with the US have already prompted many global manufacturers to switch some or all of their production facilities to other parts of Asia. Beijing is concerned that the coronavirus could expedite this trend. Yet the pandemic may even force multi-nationals to look beyond South-East Asian countries for manufacturing capacity since they are themselves reliant on China for inputs. That could open the way for the expansion of production hubs in jurisdictions such as Eastern Europe, Turkey and Mexico, as the benefits of being geographically close to China recede.

But it is not just China's prospects as an FDI recipient that have been hit by the coronavirus. The country's inevitable economic recession is likely to further squeeze its overseas-bound FDI, which at its peak in 2016 amounted to over $200 billion, nearly 2% of the country's GDP. Chinese investment flows were subsequently hit by Beijing's efforts to curb capital flight along with the emerging protectionism of some advanced economies. From 2018 China saw outward FDI drop around 50% over two years.

Protectionism

Even before the current health crisis, Chinese investment flows into Europe had experienced substantial reductions and a further decline seems likely - although some of the finance shortfall will be offset by business assistance packages. The European Bank for Reconstruction and Development has set up a one billion euro 'Solidarity Package' to help companies impacted by the pandemic across the region, and says it stands ready to do more when needed.

In March 2020 the head of the European Commission, Ursula von der Leyen, urged member states to screen potential outside investors carefully to counter takeovers of companies with reduced market capitalisation, particular those in sectors such as security, public health, medical research and strategic infrastructure. Her appeal coincided with the launch of new guidelines on the screening of inbound FDI, including the types of measures that can be taken to restrict capital movements when justified.

Von der Leyen's warning comes as a new EU-wide screening regime, aimed at safeguarding the bloc's strategic assets, is expected to be fully applied across the Union later this year.

The policy includes a new mechanism that enables member states and the Commission to exchange information and raise concerns related to specific foreign investments, especially those that are deemed to pose a threat to more than one EU country, or undermine a project or programme of interest to the bloc as a whole.

This comes as a number of European countries, seeking extra protections against foreign takeovers that potentially undermine their national interests, introduce their own inbound FDI regulations. Countries toughening their foreign investment scrutiny policies include Italy, France and Germany. German Finance Minister Olaf Scholz recently expressed concern that Beijing might exploit the pandemic to acquire more cheap European assets.

In America, where economic nationalism under President Trump has made it less accommodating than the EU to Chinese investment, efforts to vet incoming FDI deemed to threaten national interests were already increasing before the current pandemic. In 2018 Congress enacted the Foreign Investment Risk Review Modernisation Act - the most comprehensive revision of the scrutiny process for over a decade. The law widened the scope of the Committee on Foreign Investment in the United States (CFIUS), which assists the US president with reviews of transactions for potential national security risks. The reform came amid an acceleration of CFIUS's [investigative activities](#) - with much of its attention focused on acquisition bids by Chinese investors.

A worldwide FDI recovery will clearly depend on the efficacy of governmental crisis-mitigation measures, in tackling the spread of the virus and supporting business. But when that recovery comes, the foreign investment landscape may have changed markedly.

The Decoupling of "Chimerica"

When the concept of 'Chimerica' was first created (I recommend videos and books by Niall Ferguson) in 2007, it was intended to encapsulate a new world economic order that combined Chinese export-led economic growth with U.S. over-consumption. Chimerica was an unlikely financial marriage between the world's sole superpower and its most likely future rival. Behind this two-sided economic phenomenon was the integration of a massive Asian labor force and savings surplus into the world economy, which increased global returns on capital, by reducing labor costs, while depressing the cost of capital.

Thanks in large measure to its symbiotic relationship with the United States, China is now (on a current dollar basis) the second-largest economy in this world. For the United States, Chimerica meant cheaper consumer goods and lower interest rates. The global financial crisis of 2008–2009 was the beginning of the end of Chimerica. Today's Chimerica is significantly different from its 2007 antecedent. For one thing, China itself has changed. It might be said that China has increasingly come to resemble the United States, with rising levels of household consumption, higher wages, and an increasingly complex financial system characterized by shadow banking, off-balance-sheet entities, and a very large aggregate debt burden. The biggest change, however, is in the United States, leadership has taken an anti-Chinese turn. The new National Security Strategy, published in December 2017, explicitly identified China—along with Russia—as a 'strategic competitor' of the United States.

It appears that the US will achieve its objective.

The pandemic is exacerbating friction between the two countries. In Washington, many hold the Chinese government responsible, thanks to its weeks of cover-up and inaction, including failing to promptly lock down Wuhan, the city where the outbreak started, and allowing thousands of infected people to leave and spread the virus farther. China's attempt now to portray itself as offering a successful model for coping with the pandemic and to use this moment as an opportunity to expand its influence around the world will only add to American hostility. Meanwhile, nothing about the current crisis will change China's view that the U.S. presence in Asia is a historical anomaly or reduce its resentment of U.S. policy on a range of issues, including trade, human rights, and Taiwan.

The idea of "decoupling" the two economies had gained considerable traction before the pandemic, driven by fears in the United States that it was becoming too dependent on a potential adversary for many essential goods and overly susceptible to Chinese espionage and intellectual property theft. The impetus to decouple will grow as a result of the pandemic, and only in part because of concerns about China. There will be renewed focus on the potential for interruption of supply chains along with a desire to stimulate domestic manufacturing. Global trade will partly recover, but more of it will be managed by governments rather than markets.

The resistance across much of the developed world to accepting large numbers of immigrants and refugees, a trend that had been visible for at least the past half decade, will also be intensified by the pandemic. This will be in part out of concern over the risk of importing infectious disease, in part because high unemployment will make societies wary of accepting outsiders. This opposition will grow even as the number of displaced persons and refugees—already at historic levels—will continue to increase significantly.

The result will be both widespread human suffering and greater burdens on states that can ill afford them. State weakness has been a significant global problem for decades, but the economic toll of the pandemic will create even more weak or failing states. This will almost certainly be exacerbated by a mounting debt problem: public and private debt in much of the world was already at unprecedented levels, and the need for government spending to cover health-care costs and support the unemployed will cause debt to skyrocket. The developing world in particular will face enormous requirements it cannot meet, and it remains to be seen whether developed countries will be willing to provide help given demands at home. There is a real potential for aftershocks—in India, in Brazil and Mexico, and throughout Africa—that could interfere with global recovery.

The spread of COVID-19 to and through Europe has also highlighted the loss of momentum of the European project. Countries have mostly responded individually to the pandemic and its economic effects. But the process of European integration had run out of steam long before this crisis—as Brexit demonstrated especially clearly. The principal question in the post-pandemic world is how much the pendulum will continue to swing from Brussels to national capitals, as countries question whether control over their own borders could have slowed the virus's spread.

This United States is not currently disposed to take on a leading international role, the result of fatigue brought on by two long wars in Afghanistan and Iraq and rising needs at home. Even if a foreign policy "traditionalist" such as former Vice President Joseph Biden wins the November presidential election, resistance from Congress and the public will prevent the full-scale return of an expansive U.S. role in the world. And no other country, not China or anyone else, has both the desire and the ability to fill the void the United States has created.

Chapter 5 - Conclusion - The "Shut In" Economy

Take Aways:

1. Periodic lockdowns may continue from time to time. It may now be a part of life.

2. Lockdowns and social distancing have accelerated the growth of the so called "shut-in economy". Get to know that term.

3. Growth in remote working and remote learning will accelerate. Understandably those whose livelihoods are threatened by these trends are not pleased to hear this. But they would be wise to prepare anyway.

4. E-commerce will continue to boom. Think Amazon. Think food delivery services.

5. New safety measures will seem intrusive and may compromise personal data but increased surveillance will be deemed necessary. Get used to it.

6. People with reduced access to health care, or who live in more disease-prone areas, will now also be more frequently shut out of places and opportunities open to others.

7. Workers negatively impacted by the "shut-in economy" will see their situations become even more precarious. Start adapting quickly.

8. The world has changed many times, and it is changing again.

This section references an article in the Harvard Business Review called - Understanding the Economic Shock of Coronavirus by Philipp Carlsson-Szlezak, Martin Reeves and Paul Swartz.

As the coronavirus continues its march around the world, governments have turned to proven public health measures, such as social distancing, to physically disrupt the contagion. Yet, doing so has severed the flow of goods and people, stalled economies, and is in the process of delivering a global recession. Economic contagion is now spreading as fast as the disease itself.

In the previous section it was suggested that this is not a temporary disruption. It may in fact be the start of a completely different way of life.

The concept of a recession can be overly simplistic. All it says is that expectations have flipped from positive to negative growth, at least for two consecutive quarters.

We need to understand the shape of the shock — what we call "shock geometry" — and its structural legacy. What drives the economic impact path of a shock, and where does Covid-19 fit in?

To illustrate, consider how the same shock —the global financial crisis — led to recessions with vastly different progressions and recoveries in three sample countries:

- V-shape. In 2008, Canada avoided a banking crisis: Credit continued to flow, and capital formation was not as significantly disrupted. Avoiding a deeper collapse helped keep labor in place and prevented skill atrophy. GDP dropped but substantially climbed back to its pre-crisis path. This is typical of a classic "V-shape" shock, where output is displaced but growth eventually rebounds to its old path.

- U-shape. The United States had a markedly different path. Growth dropped precipitously and never rebounded to its pre-crisis path. Note that the growth rate recovered but the gap between the old and new path remains large, representing a one-off damage to the economy's supply side, and indefinitely lost output. This was driven by a deep banking crisis that disrupted credit intermediation. As the recession dragged on, it did more damage to the labor supply and productivity. The U.S. in 2008 is a classic "U-shape" — a much more costly version than Canada's V-shape.

- L-shape. Greece is the third example and by far the worst shape — not only has the country never recovered its prior output path, but also its growth rate has declined. The distance between old and new path is widening, with lost output continuously growing. This means the crisis has left lasting structural damage to the economy's supply side. Capital inputs, labor inputs, and productivity are repeatedly damaged. Greece can be seen as an example of L-shape, by far the most pernicious shape.

So, what drives "shock geometry" as shown above? The key determinant is the shock's ability to damage an economy's supply side, and more specifically, capital formation. When credit intermediation is disrupted and the capital stock doesn't grow, recovery is slow, workers exit the workforce, skills are lost, productivity is down. The shock becomes structural.

V, U, L shocks can come in different intensities. A V-shaped path may be shallow or deep. A U-shape may come with a deep drop to a new growth path or a small one.

Recession vs Depression

Take-Away

1. The debate over "recession vs depression" or "V shaped vs U shaped recovery" is somewhat academic. All that matters to internationally mobile entrepreneurs, expats and investors is that the economic contraction will be "bad"

2. We need to prepare by answering questions that include -

- Relatively speaking, which sectors and geographies will thrive vs which will struggle or disappear?

- Which residencies and citizenship should be in our portfolio as we seek to avoid unrest, protect our families and protect our wealth?

- Should we be unable to access our onshore / offshore assets due to travel restrictions, do we have power of attorney, logistics and IT structures in place to manage and access our assets?

Let's start by defining terms.

Recession: Most experts agree that a recession happens when the economy shrinks for at least two fiscal quarters in a row -- in other words, six months. This is measured by gross national product, or GDP, which is a number that represents the total value of goods and services produced within a country. However, in the US, the National Bureau of Economic Research (NBER), which officially declares recessions, says the two consecutive quarters of decline in real GDP are not how it is defined anymore. The NBER defines a recession as a significant decline in economic activity spread across the economy, lasting more than a few months, normally visible in real GDP, real income, employment, industrial production, and wholesale-retail sales.

Depression: A depression is far more uncommon and longer lasting. For example, in the last 166 years, there have been 33 recessions and only one depression. Think of a depression as two or more recessions linked together with no economic recovery in between. The Great Depression of the 1930s is the most recent and well-known example. Economic depressions last years as opposed to months.

- A depression is really dramatic. The downturn in economic activity is combined with a sharp fall in growth, employment, and production.

- Economists disagree on the duration of depressions. Some believe a depression encompasses only the period plagued by declining economic activity. Other economists argue that the depression continues up until the point that most economic activity has returned to normal.

What happens during a Depression -
- Substantial increases in unemployment - in the U.S., unemployment climbed to nearly 25 percent in 1933, remaining in the double-digits until 1941, when it finally receded to 9.66 percent.
- A drop in available credit
- Diminishing output and productivity - wages slid 42 percent, real estate prices declined 25 percent, total U.S. economic output nearly halved to $55 billion and many investors' portfolios became completely worthless.
- Consistent negative GDP growth
- Bankruptcies
- Sovereign debt defaults
- Reduced trade and global commerce
- Bear market in stocks - The United States was already in a recession, and the following Tuesday, on Oct. 29, 1929, the Dow Jones Industrial Average fell 12 percent in another mass sell-off, triggering the start of the Great Depression.
- Sustained asset price volatility and falling currency values
- Low to no inflation, or even deflation
- Increased savings rate (among those who can save)

Depression vs. Recession

The take-home lesson here is that a recession can't be defined until at least half a year has passed, and a depression can almost never be identified until after it's happened. So let's here what the experts have to say.

Ex-Fed Chairman Ben Bernanke

Ex-Fed Chairman Ben Bernanke said, on a March 2020 CNBC interview, that the coronavirus economic halt is more like a natural disaster than an economic depression. The Great Depression lasted for 12 years, and it came from human problems.

Bernanke is on the record as saying that he does expect a "very sharp" U.S. recession, but also a "fairly quick" recovery. Bernanke's comments echoed what current St. Louis Fed President James Bullard has said. Bullard believes the economy is facing a huge shock to the system over the near term, but it will then bounce back strongly after the worst of the outbreak passes.

The St. Louis Fed president and his fellow central bankers have taken extraordinary steps during the pandemic, pushing short-term borrowing rates to near zero and pledging asset purchases with no limit to support markets.

Ray Dalio of Bridgewater Associates

Bridgewater Associates is the world's largest hedge fund. Dalio sees the coming economic downturn as resembling the effects of the Great Depression. He foresees double-digit unemployment and a more than 10% decline in the economy, with effects potentially lasting years rather than months.

"I think you could look at this like a tsunami that's hit — the virus itself and the social distancing — and then what are the consequences in terms of the wreckage [from that]." He sees the "wreckage" as the long-term effects on businesses' balance sheets and individuals' incomes that are taking "tremendous" hits in cases where workers have been laid off.

Goldman Sachs has predicted that U.S. unemployment could hit 15% and a GDP decline of 34% in the second quarter of 2020. Dalio also estimated that global losses could be anywhere from $12 trillion to $20 trillion from a global economy that's worth over $85 trillion.

Dalio is not alone in bracing for the worst at the moment. Democratic presidential candidate Joe Biden has said that the economic recovery from this pandemic could be the "biggest challenge in modern history" and that it could "eclipse" what the country faced during the Great Depression.

Kristalina Georgieva, IMF Managing Director

Kristalina Georgieva calls this "A Crisis Like No Other" in a speech made in April 2020. She does not take sides however and sees the impact as worse than a recession but not quite an economic depression. Global growth is expected to turn sharply negative in 2020 and it could be the worst economic fallout since the Great Depression. Over 170 countries will experience negative per capita income growth in 2020.

The bleak outlook applies to advanced and developing economies alike. Given the necessary containment measures to slow the spread of the virus, the world economy is taking a substantial hit. This is especially true for retail, hospitality, transport, and tourism. In most countries, the majority of workers are either self-employed or employed by small and medium-sized enterprises. These businesses and workers are especially exposed. And just as the health crisis hits vulnerable people hardest, the economic crisis is expected to hit vulnerable countries hardest.

Emerging markets and low-income nations—across Africa, Latin America, and much of Asia—are at high risk. With weaker health systems to begin with, many face the dreadful challenge of fighting the virus in densely populated cities and poverty-stricken slums—where social distancing is hardly an option. With fewer resources to begin with, they are dangerously exposed to the ongoing demand and supply shocks, drastic tightening in financial conditions, and some may face an unsustainable debt burden.

They are also exposed to massive external pressure. In February and March 2020, portfolio outflows from emerging markets were about $100 billion—more than three times larger than for the same period of the 2008 global financial crisis. Commodity exporters are taking a double blow from the collapse in commodity prices. And remittances—the lifeblood of so many poor people—are expected to decline.

There is no question that 2020 will be exceptionally difficult. Assuming a gradual lifting of containment measures and reopening of the economy, a partial recovery is expected in 2021.

Where does the coronavirus shock fit in so far? The intensity of the shock will be determined by the underlying virus properties, policy responses, as well as consumer and corporate behavior in the face of adversity. But the shape of the shock is determined by the virus' capacity to damage economies' supply side, particularly capital formation. At this point, both a deep V-shape and a U are plausible. The battle ahead is to prevent a clear U trajectory.

So let us now discuss this in more practical terms. In any scenario, the short term will be hugely damaging to businesses that rely on people coming together in large numbers: restaurants, cafes, bars, nightclubs, gyms, hotels, theaters, cinemas, art galleries, shopping malls, craft fairs, museums, musicians and other performers, sporting venues (and sports teams), conference venues (and conference producers), cruise lines, airlines, public transportation, private schools, day-care centers. That is to say nothing of the stresses on parents thrust into home-schooling their kids, people trying to care for elderly relatives without exposing them to the virus, people trapped in abusive relationships, and anyone without a financial cushion to deal with swings in income.

But there would be innovation. Innovation or adaptation. Gyms could start selling home equipment and online training sessions, for example. We'll see an explosion of new services in what's already been dubbed the "shut-in economy."

Many people and companies realise that they had more to offer them than they had realised. Zoom, an online videoconferencing service is exploding. Now it is providing hundreds of millions of people a day not just with meetings, but with Tai Chi classes and "quarantinis". Slack and Microsoft's Teams are gaining many converts. No one expects the amount of distance working ever again to be as low as it was before the virus hit.

Restrictions put in place during the sars outbreak of 2003 helped accelerate China's embrace of e-commerce. Covid-19 is having a similar effect, even in economies where e-commerce is already common. Chris Grigg, boss of British Land, one of Britain's biggest retail and office landlords, says that as a result of covid-19 his company has brought forward by several years the time when it expects the share of shopping done online in Britain to double from its current 20%—already among the highest levels in the world.

The pandemic may not just highlight the convenience of online life; it may also make some of its drawbacks less disturbing. Germans, who have historically well-founded privacy concerns, are resistant to anything that looks like "surveillance capitalism". But Karl Haeusgen, chairman of hawe, a maker of hydraulic pumps, says an app that helps maintain public health by tracing covid-19 infections could make them less protective of their data. If that were the case, they might become converts to other data-driven business, too.

This trend will be good news for giants of the tech scene such as Alphabet, Amazon and Apple. So will other factors. The need for economic resilience will be added to the arguments against breaking up the biggest tech companies. If the tech world continues to splinter into rival Chinese and Western camps each side will want its champions.

As the world gets back on its feet, big firms will have better access to capital markets, giving them an extra edge over smaller competitors. And across the world there will be one increasingly big customer, too—the state. Governments will be the demand engine in many economies for the next couple years.

In the near term, we may find awkward compromises that allow us to retain some semblance of a social life. Maybe movie theaters will take out half their seats, meetings will be held in larger rooms with spaced-out chairs, and gyms will require you to book workouts ahead of time so they don't get crowded.

Ultimately, however, I predict that we'll restore the ability to socialize safely by developing more sophisticated ways to identify who is a disease risk and who isn't, and discriminating—legally—against those who are.

The world has changed many times, and it is changing again.

PostScript - Remember the End Game

This chapter is drawn from my previous book in which I proposed four (4) pillars of your international entrepreneur lifestyle. Four ideas that will put you in the driving seat when dealing with your team of advisors. For the benefit of those who have not read it before, here it is again as I believe that it is more relevant than ever before.

Inexperienced international entrepreneurs also get nervous when we discuss offshore bank accounts, foreign companies and considering tax treaties. The media reporting on scandals such as the Panama Papers, the Paradise Papers and 1MDB, sometimes paint all international structures as dishonest, unethical, illegal or immoral.

The point of this book is to put these fears and concerns to rest. Tax planning when done by a qualified team, acting honestly is completely legal. The bottom line is that the more informed you are about international tax planning, the better equipped your business will be to complete in this global economy.

(i) Flag Theory - Diversify Your Lifestyle

Idea 1 - You can diversify your lifestyle. Derisk yourself by ensuring that you and your assets are not under the control of any single jurisdiction.

For international entrepreneurs, this is key. Remember the concept of Flag Theory which was mentioned in a previous chapter. Flag Theory presents a framework for diversifying your lifestyle and your wealth.

(ii) Choose Tax Systems that Work For You

Idea 2: Death may be certain but taxes are not. You can choose where and how to be taxed by choosing where to do business and where to live.

In order to help you choose, I'll talk about how international entrepreneurs see tax systems. There are many ways of classifying tax systems. Given that we are writing for International Entrepreneurs and Expats, we have chosen to put tax systems into three (3) categories.

- In a pure worldwide tax system, resident individuals and entities are taxable on their worldwide income regardless of where the income is derived.

- By contrast, in a pure territorial tax system, the country taxes only income derived within its borders, irrespective of the residence of the taxpayer.

- A tax free jurisdiction allows resident individuals and entities to do business and pay no direct taxes on income.

That's the theory. In practice, no jurisdiction fits neatly into one of these three (3) boxes. Jurisdictions tend to be a combination of these. But I believe that it is important to think in these terms to help you decide where to plant your flags (see the section on flag theory) or where you decide to establish a presence.

Remember that your incorporated business is a separate legal entity from you as an individual. It is often subject to different tax rules from you.

So at the time of writing, in 2020, very generally speaking, tax resident individuals are subject to -

- Worldwide taxation on earned income in the USA, Canada, the UK, most of Europe, Australia and New Zealand among others;

- Territorial taxation on earned income in Hong Kong, Singapore, Malaysia, and many Caribbean islands among others;

- No tax on earned income in certain free trade zones in various jurisdictions.

When it comes to taxation, the rules are always nuanced which is why many international entrepreneurs doing their own research often get it wrong. It is possible to be -

• Tax resident in many European countries including the UK, and be taxed only on territorial income under various schemes in the UK, Portugal, Cyprus, Malta and Spain among other countries;

• Tax resident in Hong Kong and Singapore and pay taxes on income earned or dividends received from foreign sources;

• Tax resident in a free trade zone in the Philippines or Dubai but still be subject to taxes on certain types of income.

Remember your corporate structures, as legal persons, are often separate and distinct from you as a natural person. In terms of entities, the rules in a given jurisdiction can subject tax resident individuals to worldwide taxation but tax resident entities to territorial taxation. Let's have a look at corporate taxation.

- All G-7 countries including the US, "claim" to have now adopted territorial taxation (or a partial version thereof) for active business income. OECD countries claiming territorial corporate tax include - Australia, Austria, Belgium, Canada, Czech Republic, Denmark, Estonia, Finland, France, Germany, Hungary, Iceland, Italy, Japan, Luxembourg, Netherlands, New Zealand, Norway, Portugal, Slovak Republic, Slovenia, Spain, Sweden, Switzerland, Turkey, United Kingdom. I deliberately used the word "claim" because on a closer look, you would find that many of these jurisdictions have rules which do trigger worldwide corporate taxation under certain circumstances.

- Worldwide taxation is a system under which corporations deemed "resident" in a country are taxable by that country on their income from all over the world, normally with offset either by deduction or credit for taxes paid to source countries on the same income, and sometimes, with deferral of tax until repatriation of the income in the form of dividends from foreign subsidiaries to the home country resident parent. Countries with worldwide corporate taxation include jurisdictions popular with international entrepreneurs such as most Latin American nations (including Colombia), Indonesia (with 17,000 islands including Bali) and Thailand.

By now it is clear that, as an international entrepreneur, you need to be careful about where you spend your time. Even though you are a solopreneur incorporated in Estonia for example, by virtue of working from a coworking spot in Indonesia, your company may unwittingly establish a taxable presence in Indonesia and the tax authority may have the ability to levy a tax on the worldwide income of your entity.

Tread carefully. Get advice.

(iii) Choose to Live Where YOU Want

Idea 3: Most countries in the world have programs that allow foreign investors to become local residents. Others also allow investors to become citizens.

There are loads of websites that explain (and sell) residencies and citizenships. This is not necessarily illegal or unethical. Every developed country you can think of now has them as nations compete for global talent. Any team that advises international entrepreneurs needs to be familiar with economic migration options. Multiple citizenships and / or residencies now form a part of the portfolio of any international entrepreneur. It is hard to control your tax position without first taking control of your residency.

Now we will clarify these two (2) terms as they are subject to much misinterpretation. For these definitions, I will refer to the Merriam Webster dictionary.

Citizenship refers to a person's allegiance to a government in exchange for its protection at home and abroad. Full political rights, including the right to vote and to hold public office, and civil liberties are typically granted to a native-born citizen (under jus soli, a Latin legal term meaning, literally, "right of the soil") or to a naturalized citizen—i.e., a person who has successfully met official requirements that make him or her a citizen of a country other than their country of birth. (The term naturalization is of 16th-century Scottish origin.)

In a court of law, the term resident is often contrasted with citizen: it names a person who has a residence in a particular place but does not necessarily have the status of a citizen. Take, for example, an everyday occurrence in immigration law: a person who has citizenship outside of the United States and who desires to work or live in the country applies for a green card, an identification card that attests to his or her legal residence in the country as an alien—that is, a person who was born in a different country and is not a citizen of the country in which he or she now resides. He or she is not allowed to vote in, or stand for federal elections (rights which are granted to citizens); additionally, they can be subject to deportation if they commit certain crimes or security violations. After a certain period of permanent residency, an alien may apply for naturalization.

The above is simple enough but what about a variation of residency called "tax residency"?

In many countries, immigration law is separate and distinct from tax laws. So someone can, for example, enter the USA illegally and have no legal basis for being there from an immigration standpoint. But because they have spent a certain number of days there and have been working there, they may still be considered tax residents. Similarly someone can stay outside of the USA, their entire life and still be considered a tax resident there!

The point I'm making is that these rules are very nuanced. It is therefore important to understand the rules around tax residency in whichever jurisdiction you may be exposed.

(iv) You can Bank Internationally

Idea 4: You have the ability to bank internationally. But you need to see things from the bank's point of view and understand why banks are now so picky.

For international entrepreneurs, banking tends to rank about the biggest concerns. To understand why banks are becoming so hard to deal with, you need to appreciate the evolving regulatory framework. Regulations are getting stricter as a result of numerous scandals.

To get into these would be a book in itself, but in short –

- All of Europe's Top Ten banks have been fined for money laundering offences in the last decade.

- All major UK banks, including HSBC, Barclays, RBS and Standard Chartered, have been fined for money laundering offences. Earlier this year, Donald Toon, director of prosperity at the National Crime Agency (NCA), admitted in a Treasury Meeting that money laundering in the UK is "a very big problem" and estimated that the amount of money laundered each year had risen to a staggering £150 billion.

- In November 2019, Australia's financial crime watchdog accused Westpac bank of 23 million breaches of anti-money laundering and counter-terrorism financing laws.

- American banks have also been caught out. Citigroup, Wells Fargo and JP Morgan have had their share of problems and fines as well.

In addition to these fines, there are new rules around FATCA and CRS.

What is FATCA? In March 2010, the Hiring Incentives to Restore Employment (HIRE) Act introduced a new U.S. withholding and information tax regime under rules known as the Foreign Account Tax Compliance Act (FATCA). The stated purpose of the law is "to clamp down on tax evasion and improve taxpayer compliance by giving the IRS new administrative tools to detect, deter and discourage offshore tax abuses." FATCA has extensive implications including its impact on three (3) groups.

- Firstly, it affects individuals with US tax filing requirements as they now have to comply with the requirements of Form 8938 which requires reporting of taxpayer's specified foreign financial assets over certain thresholds.

- Secondly, most major governments have signed information sharing agreements (called intergovernmental agreements or IGAs) with the US which means that offshore financial information controlled by US persons will be shared.

- Thirdly, most major financial institutions based outside of the US (called foreign financial institutions or FFIs) are sharing the financial information of US persons directly with the US or indirectly via their respective governments.

Following on from FATCA, is something called CRS. The Common Reporting Standard (CRS) adopted elements of the Foreign Account Tax Compliance Act (FATCA) to create a worldwide framework for automatically sharing financial account information. Now all the major economies are determined to introduce FATCA-like intergovernmental agreements (IGAs).

There are three primary terms surrounding the Automatic Exchange of Information that need to be understood -

- The Convention on Mutual Administrative Assistance in Tax Matters (The Convention). This is a freestanding multilateral agreement designed to promote international co-operation for better operation of national tax laws, while respecting the fundamental rights of taxpayers. It covers the exchange of information, simultaneous tax examinations, tax examinations abroad, assistance in recovery and measures of conservancy, the service of documents, and joint audit facilities.

- The Competent Authority Agreement (CAA). This is the IGA version of CRS, based on the FATCA Model 1 IGA. It is a bilateral or multilateral agreement to conduct the actual Automatic Exchange of Information (AEoI).

- The Common Reporting Standard (CRS) is also known formally as the Automatic Exchange of Information (AEoI) or informally as the global version of FATCA (GATCA). This is similar to FATCA but while FATCA is implemented through IGAs, the CRS is implemented through CAA either between two countries (bilateral CAA or BCAA) or more than two countries (multilateral CAA).

The end result is that banks are facing more rules and regulations than ever before. At the same time, they are facing governments keen to charge hefty penalties for non compliance. So banks are -

- Very careful in on-boarding new account holders. Opening a bank account now feels like a job interview.

- Closing accounts with activity deemed to be suspicious.

- Avoiding business models they do not understand such as crypto and blockchain projects.

- Avoiding US exposed accounts.

- Closing accounts where the tax residency or identity of the ultimate beneficial owners is not understood.

Tax compliance and banking now go hand in hand as banks are being held responsible for actions of account holders.

www.ingramcontent.com/pod-product-compliance
Lightning Source LLC
Chambersburg PA
CBHW080510220526
45465CB00006B/2429